# CONTENTS

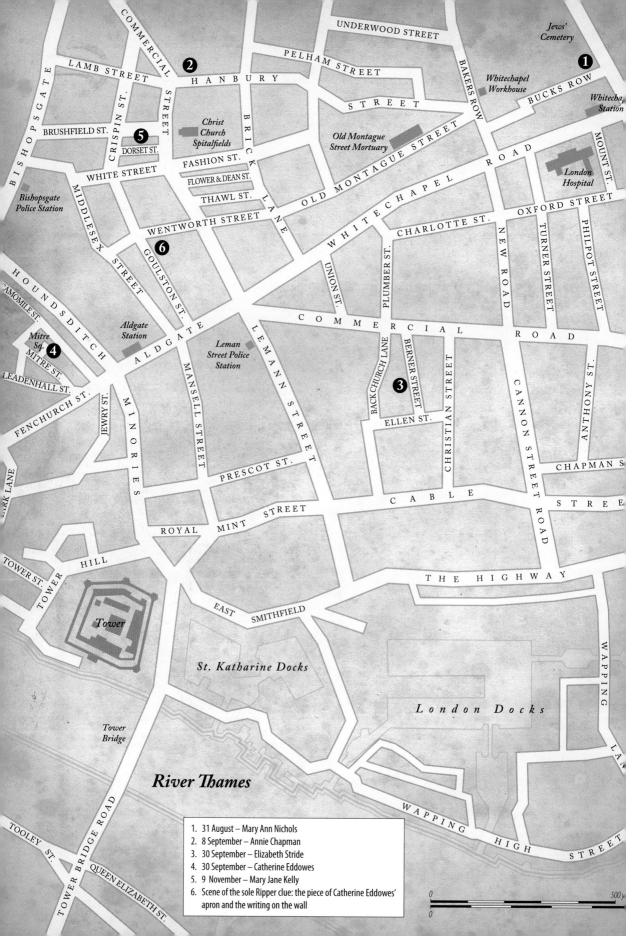

UNDERWOOD STREET

Jews' Cemetery

PELHAM STREET

COMMERCIAL

LAMB STREET

HANBURY

STREET

**②**

BAKERS ROW

BUCKS ROW

**①**

Whitechapel Workhouse

Whitecha... Station

BISHOPSGATE

BRUSHFIELD ST.

CRISPIN ST.

STREET

Christ Church Spitalfields

BRICK LANE

Old Montague Street Mortuary

OLD MONTAGUE STREET

MOUNT ST.

London Hospital

**⑤**

DORSET ST.

FASHION ST.

WHITECHAPEL

ROAD

WHITE STREET

FLOWER & DEAN ST.

Bishopsgate Police Station

THAWL ST.

CHARLOTTE ST.

NEW ROAD

OXFORD STREET

TURNER STREET

PHILPOT STREET

MIDDLESEX STREET

WENTWORTH STREET

**⑥**

GOULSTON ST.

UNION ST.

PLUMBER ST.

HOUNDSDITCH

...AMOMILE ST.

Aldgate Station

LEMAN STREET

COMMERCIAL ROAD

BACK CHURCH LANE

BERNER STREET

CHRISTIAN STREET

CANNON STREET ROAD

ANTHONY ST.

CHAPMAN S...

Mitre Sq.

**④**

Leman Street Police Station

**③**

ELLEN ST.

STREE...

MITRE ST.

LEADENHALL ST.

JEWRY ST.

ALDGATE

MANSELL STREET

...ARK LANE

FENCHURCH ST.

MINORIES

PRESCOT ST.

CABLE

STREET

ROYAL MINT STREET

THE HIGHWAY

TOWER ST.

TOWER HILL

EAST SMITHFIELD

WAPPING LAN...

Tower

St. Katharine Docks

London Docks

Tower Bridge

*River Thames*

WAPPING HIGH STREET

TOOLEY ST.

TOWER BRIDGE ROAD

QUEEN ELIZABETH ST.

1. 31 August – Mary Ann Nichols
2. 8 September – Annie Chapman
3. 30 September – Elizabeth Stride
4. 30 September – Catherine Eddowes
5. 9 November – Mary Jane Kelly
6. Scene of the sole Ripper clue: the piece of Catherine Eddowes' apron and the writing on the wall

0                                        500 y...

0

# JACK THE RIPPER

## VICTOR STAPLETON

OSPREY ADVENTURES

First published in Great Britain in 2014 by Osprey Publishing,
Midland House, West Way, Botley, Oxford, OX2 0PH, UK
44–02 23rd St, Suite 219, Long Island City, NY 11101, USA

E-mail: info@ospreypublishing.com

Osprey Publishing is part of the Osprey Group

© 2014 Osprey Publishing

A CIP catalog record for this book is available from the British Library
Print ISBN: 978 1 4728 0606 2
PDF e-book ISBN: 978 1 4728 0607 9
EPUB e-book ISBN: 978 1 4728 0608 6

# INTRODUCTION

Given the long shadow cast by Jack the Ripper over the annals of crime, it can be a surprise to learn that the killer prowled the streets of the East End for only ten short weeks in the autumn of 1888 and that his tally of murders may have been as few as five. If the crime spree was short, the reign of terror has been long. One hundred and twenty-five years on from 'The Whitechapel Murders', the figure of Jack the Ripper still haunts the popular imagination. Walking tours nightly lead tourists around what little remains of the Ripper's Whitechapel hunting ground; new or reheated theories as to the Ripper's identity regularly appear in the press and online; and Jack, complete with top hat, cape, and Gladstone bag, remains a centrepiece in both Madame Tussaud's Chamber of Horrors and the London Dungeon's recreation of dark scenes from London's past.

Why this enduring fascination with a Victorian villain? The main reason must of course be the fact that Jack's identity remains unknown. The story is the quintessential 'whodunnit', benefiting from a long parade of suspects but no conclusive evidence against any of them.

Yet the Ripper's endurance is also due to an extraordinary collision of fact and fiction. As we'll see in this book, the real story of the Ripper was infused from the start with elements from folklore, Gothic fiction, melodrama, and the sensation novel. These elements ensured that the story of the Whitechapel Murders would be remembered and retold for years to come and that the Ripper would outlive his crimes and his era as a character of legend, a *dramatis persona*.

The extraordinary process by which Jack moved from fact to fiction is the subject of this book. After a look at the crimes and the police investigation of 1888, we will examine the prime suspects in the case, then and now, before exploring the ways in which the Ripper has lived on in the popular imagination.

The book will not unmask Jack the Ripper – but it will take a good close look at the many faces we have given him, and continue to give him, through time.

Hitchcock's *The Lodger: A Story of the London Fog* (1927). The landlady extends a cautious welcome to the mysterious gentleman enquiring about her vacant upper rooms. His only luggage is a small leather bag. (AF archive / Alamy)

# CHAPTER ONE: OH, MURDER!

## The Whitechapel Murders of 1888

The crimes that started it all were undoubtedly cruel and violent, though they were fewer than we might expect given the place afforded the Ripper in the annals of crime. For there were 'five victims and five victims only' according to Sir Melville MacNaughten, assistant chief constable of the CID (Criminal Investigation Department), in his 1894 memoir of the case. Historians of the crimes, or 'Ripperologists', differ on this tally – some suggesting there were fewer victims, others more – and like much about the Ripper story, it is possible that we shall never know for sure. Our greater experience and understanding of serial killers in modern times has shown that it is common for unsolved or 'cold' cases to be linked many years after the event with a killer convicted and incarcerated for other crimes. As recently as October 2013, an attempt has been made to link the 'Yorkshire Ripper' with an unsolved murder in London in September 1979. Let us follow Sir Melville's lead and start with the canonical five murders before considering the Victorian 'cold cases' that just might have been Ripper murders.

All of the Ripper's known victims were 'unfortunates' in the parlance of the day – prostitutes living close to or even beneath the poverty line. All lived in Spitalfields and Whitechapel and, with the exception of final victim, Mary Jane Kelly, were in middle age at the time of their deaths. Recounting, however briefly, their last known movements and last recorded words not only builds up a picture of the

(Mary Evans)

6

Ripper crimes, but also gives a poignant glimpse of the fragile and vulnerable lives of East End streetwalkers in late Victorian London.

## Mary Ann Nichols
### Discovered in the early hours of Friday 31 August 1888

The first certain Ripper murder took place just as the summer of 1888 was drawing to a close. In the early hours of Friday 31 August, market porter Charles Cross was threading his way through the streets of Whitechapel to begin a long day's work. As he made his way down the dimly lit thoroughfare known as Bucks Row, he came across the body of a short, middle-aged woman, slumped against the boundary wall of some stables. Assuming the woman to be drunk or injured but alive, Cross sought the help of John Paul, a second market porter, who was approaching him warily from further along Bucks Row. Paul checked the woman for vital signs, and, finding her cold to the touch, he and Cross set off together in search of a policeman. Just minutes later, the patrol beat of Police Constable 97J John Neil brought him through Bucks Row, led him up to the same stable gateway, and placed him at the centre of one of the most iconic scenes in the history of crime. Peering into the darkness at the recumbent shape on the pavement, Neil shone his bull lantern onto the body of Mary Ann Nichols, thus revealing the first certain victim of Jack the Ripper, blood oozing from a deep gash in her throat.

The identity of this first Ripper victim, and the full extent of her injuries, would only become clear over the course of that last Friday in August. After a brief examination *in situ* by Dr Rees Ralph Llewellyn of Whitechapel Road, the body was conveyed to a nearby mortuary where Dr Llewellyn's more detailed

HE SAW A BODY ON THE PAVEMENT.

(Mary Evans)

examination and autopsy revealed severe mutilation to the abdominal and pubic regions. Examination of the woman's clothing and few personal effects implied a connection with Lambeth Workhouse and suggested she had most recently been living in a local common lodging house or 'dosshouse'. Enquiries along these lines soon brought positive identification of the body as that of Mary Ann or 'Polly' Nichols, who had indeed spent stints in the Lambeth Workhouse and whose most recent address was Wilmott's Lodging House at 18 Thrawl Street, Whitechapel. It was the need to procure her four pence 'doss' money that had taken Polly out on to the dark streets of the East End the previous night. She had been optimistic of finding it, boasting to friends that a new addition to her apparel would pay dividends – 'See what a jolly bonnet I've got now'. The last recorded sightings of Polly were her drunken exit from The Frying Pan pub in Brick Lane, at 12.30 a.m., and her drunken adieu to lodging house roommate Emily Holland at the corner of Brick Lane and Whitechapel High Street at about 2.30 a.m.

The investigations at the mortuary concluded with the positive identification of Polly's body by her estranged husband William Nichols, who reportedly took his solemn leave of her with the words 'Seeing you as you are now, I forgive you for what you have done to me'. His words as he left the mortuary are also recorded: 'It has come to a sad end at last' – an end made complete a few days later when 'Polly' Nichols was laid to rest in Ilford Cemetery.

The Bucks Row murder provoked attention and feverish interest from the outset. Murder was not uncommon in the East End; violence against sex workers at the hands of clients, pimps, or the curiously named 'High Rip' or protection gangs was all too frequent. Yet the elements of the Bucks Row murder – the severity of the attack, the mutilation, the placement of the body on a public highway for all to see – stood out as different. Police and press attention was drawn to recent unsolved murders in the East End and tentative links were made with the murders of prostitutes Martha Tabram on 8 August and Emma Elizabeth Smith in April (the latter was almost certainly a victim of gang violence rather than the Ripper). The ensuing inquest, press speculation, and the public reaction to this and the following murders all served to heighten the sense that something sinister and extraordinary was unfolding in the East End: the long summer of 1888 was giving way to an autumn of terror.

## Annie Chapman
### Discovered in the early hours of Saturday 8 September 1888
While the first body was discovered on a public thoroughfare, the second would be found in the back yard of a terraced house. 29 Hanbury Street was another of the East End's many shared houses, occupied in autumn 1888 by no fewer than 17 citizens. Access to the different floors of the property was via a passage that ran the full length of the building from the Hanbury Street frontage to

a small yard at the back. Subsequent inquest testimony would reveal that this yard was regularly used by East End prostitutes and their clients – a source of annoyance to some of the Hanbury Street tenants. It was in this yard that the body of the second Ripper victim, Annie Chapman, was found early in the morning of 8 September 1888. The discovery was made by John Davis, tenant of 29 Hanbury Street, at 5.45 a.m. (he was certain as to the time as he noted the bell chimes of the nearby Christchurch, Spitalfields). Davis found the second Ripper victim lying on her back in the yard, her head towards the three steps leading from house to yard and her dress pulled up above her knees. Her throat had been cut and she too had suffered savage mutilation: this second Ripper victim had been disembowelled, displaced intestines lying over her left shoulder.

This second victim was soon identified as Annie Chapman, or 'Siffey' (she had lived for a while with a maker of iron sieves), latterly of Crossingham's Lodging House at 35 Dorset Street. In the early hours of 8 September, Tim Donovan, deputy of Crossingham's, had encountered 47-year-old Annie in the lodging-house kitchen, apparently fragile from the effects of fatigue, drink, and a recent fist fight with fellow resident Eliza Cooper, with whom she had quarrelled over a client. Donovan asked Annie for her doss money. She could not provide it but set out to procure it, first telling him, 'Don't let the bed. I'll be back soon', and then the watchman, 'See that Tim keeps the bed for me'.

Annie was never to return to claim her bed. Within 45 minutes of the gruesome discovery in Hanbury Street, Annie's body was examined *in situ* by Dr George Bagster Phillips. Observed by a growing crowd, the body was then transported to Whitechapel Workhouse Infirmary Mortuary off Old Montague Street, where Annie would later be positively identified by her friend Amelia Palmer. She would be laid to rest a week later at Manor Park Cemetery in Ilford.

This second Whitechapel murder in the space of a week provoked widespread interest and unease in the East End, something exacerbated by press speculation and by the high-profile inquests into the deaths of Mary Ann Nichols and Annie Chapman. The Hanbury Street murder site became a spectacle in itself, residents of the overlooking dwellings charging curious sightseers for a glimpse of the fateful spot – thus starting a tradition of Ripper murder-site tourism that continues to this day. It was becoming clear that a serial murderer was at large in the East End, that a significant section of the population of Whitechapel and Spitalfields was at risk, and that the odds were high that he would soon kill again.

## Elizabeth Stride and Catherine Eddowes
### Discovered in the early hours of Sunday 30 September 1888

The Ripper's third and fourth victims were claimed in a single night, unleashing a wave of hysteria across the East End and provoking unprecedented press coverage and feverish speculation. The early hours of Sunday 30 September 1888 were to witness 'the double event' – a phrase from one of the most famous of the hoax letters sent to the press and police during the Ripper scare. 'The double event' saw the murders of Elizabeth Stride and Catherine Eddowes, apparently within as little as 45 minutes of each other.

The body of third Ripper victim Elizabeth Stride was discovered within minutes of her death. Indeed, the killer may have been interrupted. Stride was found in a small courtyard adjoining the International Working Men's Club

Kate Eddowes.

in Berner Street, Whitechapel. Shortly after 1 a.m., club steward and costermonger Louis Diemschutz was returning from a long day's trading. As he ushered his pony and barrow into the court, the pony shied away from an obstruction on the ground. It is a measure of just how dark the East End streets were by night that, like those who had found the previous victims, Diemschutz could at first not make out exactly what the obstruction was. The light of a match, quickly snuffed out by the autumn wind, established that it was the body of a drunk or dead woman. The steadier flicker of a candle, hastily snatched from inside the club, established that the woman was indeed dead, a fatal gash in her throat. But that was all. No mutilations; none of the abdominal wounds associated with the Ripper's *modus operandi*. It seems the killer had been disturbed. He may have been hiding in the shadows while Diemschutz lit his match, and he may have slipped quietly from the court while Diemschutz rushed into the club for the candle.

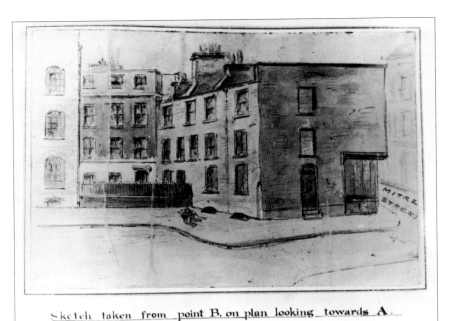

Sketch taken from point B. on plan looking towards A.

Mitre Square, scene of the murder of Catherine Eddowes. The murder spot was in plain view of the bedroom window of City Police Constable Richard Pearce: he and his family heard no disturbance that night. (Mary Evans)

Whilst Diemschutz and his companions were busy raising the alarm and calling the police to Berner Street, the next dark chapter of the Ripper saga was already unfolding. Mitre Square, the setting for the fourth murder, was situated not in Whitechapel or Spitalfields but on the edge of the City of London, that square-mile section of the capital governed since medieval times by a Lord Mayor and his Aldermen, and policed, since 1839, not by the Metropolitan Police but by a dedicated City of London police force. It was into this part of London that 46-year-old streetwalker Catherine Eddowes had drunkenly wandered shortly after 1 a.m. on the morning of 30 September 1888. Earlier that night she had been safe enough – after being found drunk on a pavement in Aldgate, she had been escorted to a cell in Bishopsgate Police Station to sober up. She was deemed sufficiently sober to be discharged at approximately 1 a.m. by Police Constable George Hutt, who took the opportunity to reprove her for drinking but who nevertheless received the affectionate 'All right. Good night, old cock' in response.

She was discovered by a City policeman on his beat. At approximately 1.45 a.m. PC Edward Watkins passed through the square, as he had only 15 minutes previously, and found the body of the Ripper's fourth victim in the south-west (and darkest) corner. On the poor victim's body were all those signature features of a Ripper killing that Elizabeth Stride's murder had lacked: the mutilation, the disembowelling, the disarrayed clothing. Indeed, the mutilations inflicted on Catherine were the worst yet, now extending to the face, where the nose had been cut and the eyelids nicked.

The discovery sent Watkins reeling into the nearby Kearley and Tonge's warehouse where he called to night watchman George Morris, 'For God's sake,

mate, come to my assistance'. Morris, raising the alarm with his whistle, fetched two additional constables, and soon medical men were also in attendance, Dr George Sequeira to pronounce death, Dr Frederick Gordon Brown to examine the body *in situ* (Brown's detailed report on the crime and sketch of the murder scene will be considered in Chapter Two). The body was soon conveyed to Golden Lane Mortuary, where fuller examination of this most violent Ripper crime to date, and identification of the murdered woman as Catherine Eddowes, would shortly follow.

Elements of Catherine Eddowes' story bring home to us anew the tragedy of the Ripper victims' lives. Consider the cruel twists of fate (and indeed of economic necessity) that had led her into harm's way. Only two days before she met her fate in Mitre Square, Catherine had been in Kent with her partner John Kelly, picking the autumnal harvest of hops as an alternative means of income. Had she stayed a further day she would not have been back in London, spending the remainder of that income on drink on Saturday 29 September. Then again, had she been just a little more drunk and slept a little longer in Bishopsgate Police Station, she would not have wandered off into the night at precisely the moment that the killer, frustrated at the interrupted attack on Elizabeth Stride, was in search of a fresh victim. One more night in Kent, one more hour in the police cell – on such small details hangs a life.

By the time Catherine Eddowes was interred in Ilford Cemetery on 8 October 1888, the impact of the Whitechapel Murders on the whole of London and beyond was approaching fever pitch. Mitre Square and the other murder sites had become a focus for dark tourism, the press was awash with theories, potential sightings, and leader articles criticising the police, and, most significantly of all, the killer now had a name, courtesy of a widely publicized letter sent to the Central News Agency on 29 September and signed 'Jack the Ripper'.

## Mary Jane Kelly
### Discovered in the early hours of Friday 9 November 1888

The final victim was murdered in her own home. Twenty-five-year-old Mary Jane Kelly lived in cramped Miller's Court, off Dorset Street, one of the most notorious of the 'mean streets' of the East End in 1888. Number 13 Miller's Court was a small, single-room dwelling, created by the partitioning of the ground floor back room of number 26 Dorset Street. The room was accessed through a doorway that led directly to the street, under the arched entrance to Miller's Court. A bed, chair, and two tables were all the furniture the room contained. A sash window gave a view onto the court and was latterly a source of constant ventilation – Mary having recently broken a pane when drunk.

The sparsely furnished single room cost Mary 4/6 (four shillings and sixpence) per week in rent payable to landlord John McCarthy, who ran a grocer's shop on the opposite side of Dorset Street. Mary would find this sum

**OPPOSITE:**
The height of the Ripper scare – the weekend of the 'double event' – saw two women murdered, the East End in panic, and the 'Whitechapel Murderer' renamed for all time as 'Jack the Ripper'.

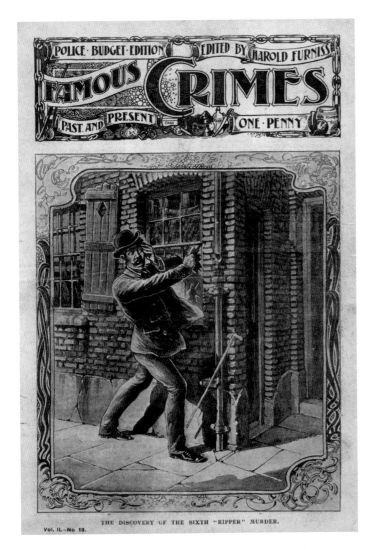

POLICE · BUDGET · EDITION    EDITED BY HAROLD FURNISS

FAMOUS CRIMES

PAST AND PRESENT    ONE · PENNY

THE DISCOVERY OF THE SIXTH "RIPPER" MURDER.

Vol. II.—No 18.

Thomas Bowyer's horrifying discovery in Miller's Court. (Mary Evans)

by assignations with clients picked up in the East End streets or in the nearby Ten Bells Pub, in which she regularly drank. Until recently, Kelly had been sharing 13 Miller's Court with on-off partner Joe Barnett – the pair had been 'off' again since Kelly had invited fellow prostitute Maria Harvey to stay with them in the already cramped dwelling. Maria had been staying with Kelly right up until the week of her death, visiting the room and leaving a pile of clothing there on the afternoon of Thursday 8 November. But by nightfall Mary had the room to herself and scope to entertain a client in the relative warmth and comfort of home rather than on the chilly streets of Whitechapel. She had pressing need of clients, the rent being in arrears and collection imminent.

It was the rent collector who found Mary, in one of the most disturbing scenes in the entire Ripper saga. Thomas Bowyer resided at 37 Dorset Street, supplementing his army pension by working for Mary's landlord, John McCarthy. To Bowyer fell the task of collecting Mary's rent on that November morning in 1888. At 10.45 a.m. he crossed into Miller's Court and knocked at the door of number 13. Receiving no answer and unable to open the apparently locked door, Bowyer reached through the broken window pane and tried to move aside the coat and curtain that were obscuring the view. He revealed a horrifying scene. The remains of the final victim of Jack the Ripper were lying on the bed, blood staining the sheets around it. The body had been mutilated beyond recognition – flesh having been cut from the face, the torso, and the thighs – and had been disembowelled and eviscerated beyond even the horrors of the Mitre Square murder. Flesh and organs had been removed and placed on the bed and the table beside it. Miller's Court had been the scene of the most depraved of the Ripper's crimes, leaving a traumatic and indelible impression upon all who witnessed it. Hardened policeman Walter Dew, the man who would later catch the notorious Dr Crippen, could never afterwards recall the case without suffering a haunting vision of the scene.

The jurors at the subsequent inquest were spared a full view of the body, as the draping of a grey sheet left only the mutilated head exposed, but even this sight made a profound impression, *The Pall Mall Gazette* likening the corpse to 'one of those horrible wax anatomical specimens'.

There was to be a delay accessing this final murder site – having secured the scene, police deferred entering 13 Miller's Court for over two hours while waiting to ascertain whether bloodhounds, recently procured by the force, might be employed to track the murderer from the scene. The hounds did not arrive (after some ineffective trials tracking Sir Charles Warren, Commissioner of the Metropolitan Police in 1888, in Hyde Park, they had been sent back to their owner), but a photographer did, taking the only *in situ* crime scene photographs associated with the Jack the Ripper case. The body was given a preliminary examination on the bed by Dr George Bagster Phillips and then transferred for post mortem to the mortuary at Shoreditch, where the inquest on Mary Jane Kelly would open the following Monday.

And although no one could have known it at the time, this was the end. There would be no more Ripper murders in 1888, and while there would be scares, speculation, and more fatal assaults on prostitutes in the years that immediately followed, November 1888 almost certainly saw the last of the Jack the Ripper murders.

Modern knowledge of serial murder teaches us that this abrupt halt to the murders is significant. While it is known for a serial killer to 'go to ground' for a spell, it is extremely rare for such a criminal to desist from murder completely. The sudden end to the Ripper murders could only mean one thing: he was no longer in a position to perpetrate the crimes. He had been incarcerated, incapacitated, or he had died.[1] This fact should be borne in mind when reviewing the parade of suspects that has been brought before us over the last 125 years. Those who were at liberty well beyond the fateful date of 9 November 1888 deviate at once from the profile we can reliably associate with a serial killer like the Ripper.

Such are the facts concerning the Jack the Ripper murders. Over a period of ten weeks Whitechapel had been terrorized by a killer who had perpetrated five horrific crimes, apparently vanishing without a trace. The killer seemed to be one step ahead of his pursuers at every turn: while those who hunted him fumbled their way through the darkness, the Ripper not only continued his crimes but orchestrated aspects of their reception, laying out the poor victims at the crime scenes for maximum shock effect. Far from concealing his victims' bodies, the Ripper left them in plain view on public thoroughfares, ready to be illuminated by the glare of a police lantern as if

---

1.  Suggestions that the Ripper might have moved away and recommenced the killings elsewhere lie behind some of the 'American doctor' Ripper theories, but this departs from what we know of the typical serial killing profile, which generally finds murderers operating close to home.

## ANOTHER RIPPER VICTIM? MARTHA TABRAM

Did the 'autumn of terror' in fact begin on 7 August 1888? It was early on this date that the body of Martha Tabram was discovered in a stairwell in George Yard Buildings, not far from Whitechapel High Street, by dock worker John Saunders Reeves. The body was examined by Dr Timothy Killeen, who found 39 stab wounds to the torso, abdomen, and pubic region.

Was this a Ripper crime? The MO (*modus operandi*) was somewhat different. First there were the stab wounds rather than the jagged slashing wounds associated with later murders; then there was the murder weapon, which the doctor considered might have been a penknife and in the case of one wound a bayonet (a detail that resonates with the apparent sighting of Martha with a soldier). But the locality of the crime and the victim's demographic was the same – 39-year-old Martha was living in a common lodging house in George Street, Spitalfields, and supplemented her small income from selling trinkets by sex-work – and some members of the press and police at the time certainly counted Martha's murder as an early Ripper crime. As with much in the Ripper case, we will never know for sure. Over 125 years later, the murder of Martha Tabram remains a Victorian cold case.

the scenes were indeed vignettes in a living Chamber of Horrors staged on the streets of Whitechapel.[2]

There had been few clues to hold on to: a few possible sightings of the victims with clients shortly before their deaths; a cry of 'No!' overheard in Hanbury Street on the night of Annie Chapman's murder; and a low cry of 'Oh, murder!' faintly made out in the early hours by Mary Kelly's Dorset Street neighbour on the night of her death. Just what the inquests, the press, and the police could make of these few clues is the story of Chapter Two.

---

2. Sure enough, at the height of the murders a small waxwork museum on the Whitechapel Road did indeed mock up the Ripper's crime scenes for a paying public.

# CHAPTER TWO: THE INQUESTS

Five murders in three months. Who, if anyone, had seen the murderer and what physical clues, if any, did he leave for the police to follow? A famous Victorian sketch from *Punch* magazine showed a Victorian bobby engaged in a game of 'Blind Man's Buff' – snatching at random for suspects and groping in the dark for leads. This was not quite fair. There were some definite lines of enquiry emerging early in the case, and the inquests on the five victims confirmed that there were indeed potential sightings and a small number of physical clues.

## The Inquest on Mary Ann Nichols

The inquest on the first Ripper victim opened on Saturday 1 September 1888. Held at the Working Lads' Institute on the Whitechapel Road, it was presided over by Coroner Wynne E. Baxter, who would oversee three of the inquests in the Ripper case. A flamboyant, almost Dickensian figure, Baxter would make his own contribution to the high drama of the case, occasionally sharing his views with the press and apparently feeling at liberty to expound his own theories as to the murderer's motivations and actions.

**BLIND-MAN'S BUFF.**
(As played by the Police.)
"TURN ROUND THREE TIMES, AND CATCH WHOM YOU MAY!"

(Mary Evans)

Witnesses at the inquest included Nichols's father, who confirmed her identity; PC John Neil, who recounted his discovery of the body; and Dr Llewellyn, who gave his account of his examination of the body *in situ* and the subsequent post mortem. Dr Llewellyn confirmed that the murder had been done:

> with a long-bladed knife, moderately sharp, and used with great violence [. . .]
> The wounds were from left to right, and might have been done by a left-handed person. All the injuries had been done by the same instrument.

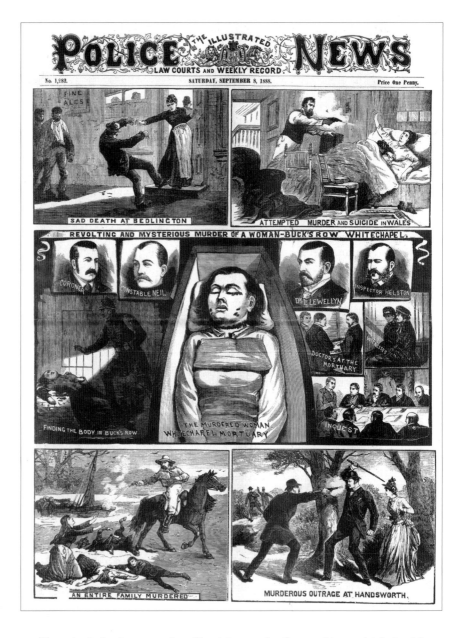

There had also been marks of bruising to the face and jaw, which, in this as in subsequent killings, suggested the victim might have been strangled before the knife wounds were inflicted.

A number of witnesses were called who lived in or nearby to Bucks Row and who might reasonably be expected to have heard this violent murder take place – none of them had. An apparently frustrated Coroner Baxter could not resist a jibe at the Winthorpe Street night watchman, who admitted to dozing on the night of the murder: 'I suppose your watching is not up to much'.

The Nichols inquest also saw some recriminations over the destruction of physical evidence in the case, in particular the washing of the body by the two mortuary attendants at the workhouse infirmary before a full medical examination had been completed.

It is striking that even at this 'first' Ripper inquest, nerves were strained and connections were being forged with earlier Whitechapel murders. A strong sense already prevailed that a serial killer was at large in the East End. The foreman of the jury, no less, reproached the police for not having offered a reward after the unsolved murder of Martha Tabram on 7 August, urging that such a reward would help the community to 'find out the monster in their midst, who was terrorizing everybody and making people ill. There were four horrible murders remaining undiscovered'. Coroner Baxter reiterated the official position that rewards were not offered in cases of this kind (the misinformation and attention-seeking generated by rewards had caused them to be discontinued since 1884). The inquest closed on Saturday 22 September 1888, establishing no obvious motive for the crime and recording a verdict of wilful murder against some person or persons unknown.

## The Inquest on Annie Chapman

Annie Chapman's inquest was held at the same venue under the same coroner, who by now had got into his stride in terms of pronouncing his own views on the case. The first witnesses called by Coroner Baxter confirmed the dead woman's immediate history and circumstances: her friend and confidante Amelia Palmer relating how she had become separated from her late husband and three children; the lodging house deputy Timothy Donovan confirming his ejection of Annie from Crossingham's on the night of her death on account

THE FRONT OF 29, HANBURY STREET.

THE REAR OF 29, HANBURY STREET.
(The + shows where the body was found.)

A contemporaneous sketch of the back yard of 29 Hanbury Street. The Annie Chapman inquest received evidence from Albert Cadoche that he had heard a cry of 'No!' and a thud against the wooden fence at the time of the murder. (Mary Evans)

of her lacking her 'doss money'; the lodging house watchman concurring the time at which she left Crossingham's and stumbled off into the night. There was just one more sighting of Annie, possibly in the company of her killer. About 5.30 a.m. on 8 September, Elizabeth Darrell or Long (the police file records both names) saw a man and a woman standing on the pavement outside 29 Hanbury Street. She had been close enough to hear a snippet of conversation: 'Will you?' (from the man); 'Yes' (from the woman). She had later identified the body of Annie in the mortuary as the woman she had seen. Mrs Long shared a description of the man she had seen, characterizing him as 'a foreigner' of 'shabby genteel' appearance, aged over 40 and wearing a dark coat and deerstalker hat.

Finally, the inquest heard that Mr Albert Cadoche, resident of the neighbouring 27 Hanbury Street, had been outside in the yard at 5.30 on the fateful morning when he had overheard the cry 'No!' and heard the thud of something falling against the fence marking the boundary of the two properties. Cadoche had not been prompted to investigate further, and leaving the yard only a couple of minutes later, he had set off for work down an empty Hanbury Street.

The medical evidence at the Chapman inquest was presented by Dr George Bagster Phillips, who was reluctant to speak of the 'wounds on the lower part of the body'. Coroner Baxter was insistent that the court should have 'all the evidence before us', but spared the sensibilities of the ladies and newspaper boys present by having them retire from the courtroom. Bagster Phillips went on to relate the detail of the mutilations (later reproduced in the medical journal *The Lancet*), complete with the macabre detail that the reproductive organs had been removed:

No trace of these parts could be found [ ... ] Obviously the work was that of an expert – of one, at least, who had such knowledge of anatomical or pathological examinations as to secure the pelvic organs with one sweep of the knife.

The Chapman inquest apparently did not hear all of the crime scene evidence associated with the murder. According to press reports and subsequent statements by two police officials, the contents of Annie's pocket had been placed rather deliberately and neatly either at her feet or beside her body. Uncertainty as to the nature, number, and exact arrangement of the objects has played a part in escalating subsequent Ripper theories involving elements of conspiracy or ritual murder, but the most reliable indications are that the objects simply comprised a piece of muslin, two hair combs, and two polished farthings. Near Annie's head had been a torn section of envelope bearing the seal of the Sussex regiment, the letter 'M' and a post office stamp from late August 1888. The envelope contained two pills – perhaps verifying Annie's claim to Tim Donovan that she had recently been ill. The final physical clue at the Chapman crime scene was the presence of a wet leather apron, lying a short

The *Illustrated Police News* reflects the gathering momentum of events in the run up to the final murder. (Lordprice Collection / Alamy)

distance from a water tap in the yard where the body lay. The significance of this object was to be magnified by subsequent events, as Chapter Four's review of suspects of the day will show.

Wynne Baxter's summing up at the Chapman inquest was to make a deep impression on the subsequent image of the Ripper in the popular consciousness. Picking up on Bagster Phillips' view that the murderer possessed medical or at least anatomical knowledge, Baxter proposed, apparently based on his own musings, that the killer was not a lunatic but a rogue medical man, seeking to procure anatomical specimens for sale (an American doctor had apparently recently inquired after specimens at the London Hospital and had been turned away). The theory was soon discredited, but it is difficult to overstate the part it played in cementing the image of Jack the gentleman doctor in the popular consciousness.

## The Inquests on the 'Double Event' – Elizabeth Stride and Catherine Eddowes

The 'double event' murders took place over two district authority areas, and thus the inquests were overseen by two different coroners. Wynne Baxter presided over his third and final Ripper case, that of Elizabeth Stride, starting on 1 October, while the inquest on Catherine Eddowes was convened by Coroner Samuel Frederick Langham on 4 October. Both inquests considered evidence of sightings of the victims, potentially in the company of their killer, on the night of their deaths. Indeed, the evidence presented at these inquests and in concurrent press accounts served to highlight just how compressed the timeline of the 'double event' had been and just how close the Ripper must have been to discovery and capture.

- **11.00 p.m.** While Catherine Eddowes is sleeping off her drunken stupor in Bishopsgate Police Station, two witnesses see Elizabeth Stride leave the Bricklayers Arms with a young man and walk in the direction of Commercial Road and Berner Street.
- **11.45 p.m.** William Marshall notices Stride with an Englishman in Berner Street. At much the same time grocer Matthew Packer sells a pound and a half of black grapes to a man accompanying a woman he believes to be Stride.
- **12.15 a.m.** Catherine Eddowes is now awake and singing softly in her cell.
- **12.30 a.m.** Police Constable William Smith sees Stride still in Berner Street, opposite Dutfield's Yard.
- **12.45 a.m.** James Brown believes he sees Stride in Fairclough Street. In a contradictory sighting, Israel Schwartz witnesses Stride being assaulted and thrown to the pavement in the entrance to Dutfield's Yard. Her assailant shouts 'Lipski!' across the road (addressed either as an insult to Schwartz or possibly as a call to another man standing nearby).[3]
- **1 a.m.** Catherine Eddowes is discharged from Bishopsgate Police Station and heads out into the night, while Louis Diemschutz discovers the body of Elizabeth Stride in Berner Street.
- **1.30 a.m.** Police Constable Edward Watkins patrols Mitre Square on his beat and sees nothing untoward.

---

3. Israel Lipski, a Polish Jewish immigrant, had been executed in 1887 for the murder by poisoning of a woman sharing his lodgings. It is generally believed that the use of his name during the Stride assault was as an anti-Semitic insult to discourage the curious onlooker Schwartz.

- **1.35 a.m.** Joseph Lawende, Joseph Hyam Levy, and Harry Harris, walking past Duke's Place in a group, all see Eddowes at the entrance to Church Passage leading into Mitre Square. She is talking intimately to a man, her hand on his chest.
- **1.40 a.m.** Police Constable James Harvey patrols Duke's Place and Church Passage on his beat; he sees no one and hears no noise from the square.
- **1.45 a.m.** Police Constable Edward Watkins enters the square from Mitre Street and finds the mutilated body of Catherine Eddowes.

That the timeline of the 'double event' was so very tight makes it all the more remarkable that the killer had time to inflict such severe mutilations on the body of Catherine Eddowes in the darkest corner of Mitre Square that night. The details of those horrendous injuries were reported in full at her inquest by Dr Frederick Gordon Brown, Surgeon to the City of London Police. Brown had conducted his *in situ* examination of the body and subsequent post mortem with meticulous care: there was none of the casual washing of the body prior to examination or other blunders that had provided cause for recrimination at earlier inquests. His very detailed report catalogued each of the horrific mutilations, from the savage abdominal slashing to the apparently delicate nicking of the eyelids and cheeks. Brown's report also confirmed that despite the pitch darkness of Mitre Square the killer had somehow located and retrieved organs from the bloody mess he had created, taking away the left kidney and the womb. The conclusion Brown drew from this has been profoundly influential in subsequent Ripper theories:

> I believe the perpetrator of the act must have had considerable knowledge of the positions of the organs in the abdominal cavity and the way of removing them. [ . . . ] It required a great deal of anatomical knowledge to have removed the kidney and to know where it was placed.

A firm basis was hereby laid for the view that the killer was a doctor or medical student, perhaps working close by at the London Hospital in Whitechapel: a respectable gentleman medic by day and a fiend by night. Such an inference was not inevitable – indeed, Brown went on to say that the anatomical knowledge displayed could have been held by 'someone in the habit of cutting up animals'. But the striking notion of a deranged doctor struck too deep for Brown's caveat to register, and one of the most enduring images of Jack the Ripper was thus frozen in aspic.

The Eddowes inquest also heard details of the major topographical clue in the Jack the Ripper case. Shortly after the murder, a piece of Catherine Eddowes' apron, stained with blood, had been discovered in Goulston Street, indicating the direction in which the killer had fled – north-easterly, back towards Whitechapel. The discovery was made by Police Constable Alfred Long in the doorway of numbers 106–199 Model Dwellings (buildings constructed by philanthropic organisations). Chalked on the wall in the covered entrance to the building was the message 'The Juwes are the men who will not be blamed for nothing'. The import of these words and their possible connection to the case has been variously debated in the 125 years since. Was this a message from the killer, designed to implicate the Jewish community in the crimes? Was it an unrelated piece of graffiti that simply happened to be on the wall of the very doorway into which the Ripper chose to discard the piece of apron? Did the curious spelling 'Juwes' reflect the poor literacy of the writer, or was it a deliberate reference not to the 'Jews' but to the 'Juwes' of Masonic tradition, who, according to Masonic legend, committed a vile murder in the precincts of their temple, mutilating their high priest in a manner strikingly similar to the injuries inflicted on Ripper victims? No certain answers have ever emerged, but the 'Goulston Street graffito' has certainly played its part in many a subsequent theory as to the Ripper's identity. And if the writing was indeed a physical trace of the Ripper it was a short-lived one: police erased the words at approximately 5.30 a.m. on that September morning before a photograph could be taken to preserve them for posterity.

The 'double event' inquests duly drew to a close, amidst increasingly feverish speculation and melodramatic press coverage. Both inquests returned their inevitable verdict of wilful murder against some person or persons unknown.

## The Inquest on Mary Jane Kelly

The inquest on the last victim, Mary Jane Kelly, was convened on 12 November at Shoreditch Town Hall by Dr Roderick MacDonald. Proceedings were concluded in a single day despite the presentation of a welter of evidence, including the detailed medical evidence deposed by Dr Thomas Bond. Given that Mary had been killed indoors rather than out on the street like her fellow victims, it was striking that this last inquest and the concurrent press reports were awash with witness statements and apparent sightings of the victim.[4]

Mary Ann Cox, of number 5 Miller's Court, deposed that she had last seen Mary at 11.45 p.m. on 8 November in company with a stout man with a blotchy face and 'carrotty' moustache: 'He had on a longish coat, very shabby, and carried a pot of ale in his hand'. Poignantly, the witness also recalled hearing Mary singing in her room later that same night – the wistful tune of 'Only a violet I plucked from my mother's grave' had stayed in her mind. Meanwhile, Elizabeth Prater of number 20 Miller's Court reported hearing

---

4. The fact that the last of these reported sightings took place after Mary is known to have died suggests that some of these statements were prompted by a wish for association with the increasingly sensational Ripper case.

a less harmonious sound – a cry of 'Oh, murder!' apparently emanating from the court between 3.30 and 4 a.m.

Sarah Lewis, a laundress of 24 Great Pearl Street, deposed having seen not Kelly, but a stout man wearing dark clothes and a 'wideawake' hat, apparently keeping vigil outside Miller's Court – 'he seemed to be waiting or looking for someone'. Caroline Maxwell of 14 Dorset Street also claimed to have seen a strange stout man in dark clothes, this one talking to Kelly outside the Britannia public house. The sighting remains one of the mysteries of the Ripper case, the witness timing it between 8.30 and 9 a.m., long after Kelly must have been dead. Pressed at the inquest, the witness stuck doggedly to her guns: 'I am sure it was the deceased. I am willing to swear it'.

There was to be one further reported sighting – this one remarkably detailed and precise, and deposed not at the inquest but at Commercial Street Police Station on the evening the Kelly inquest closed. George Hutchinson, an unemployed groom and labourer, appears to have known Kelly fairly well: he claimed to the police that she would sometimes borrow money from him and it seems a reasonable inference that he was an occasional client. He appears to have taken a very close interest in Kelly and in the gentleman she paired off with that November evening. The remarkably detailed witness statement he volunteered to the police was as follows:

A Short Stout Man.

Mary Ann Cox's suspect: 'a stout man, shabbily dressed'. (Mary Evans)

About 2.00 a.m. [on the] 9th I was coming by Thrawl Street, Commercial Street, and just before I got to Flower and Dean Street, I met the murdered woman Kelly, and she said to me, 'Hutchinson, will you lend me Sixpence?' I said, 'I can't, I've spent all my money going down to Romford', she said, 'Good morning, I must go and find some money'.

She went away toward Thrawl Street. A man coming in the opposite direction to Kelly tapped her on the shoulder and said something to her; they both burst out laughing. I heard her say, 'Alright', to him, and the man said, 'You will be alright for what I have told you'. He then placed his right hand around her shoulders. He also had a kind of a small parcel in his left hand, with a kind of strap round it.

I stood against the lamp of the Queen's Head public house and watched him.

They both came past me, and the man hung down his head with his hat over his eyes. I stooped down and looked him in the face. He looked at me stern.

They both went into Dorset Street. I followed them. They both stood at the corner of the court for about three minutes. He said something to her, she said, 'Alright my dear, come along, you will be comfortable'. He then placed his arm on her shoulder and [she] gave him a kiss. She said she had lost her handkerchief. He then pulled his handkerchief, a red one, out and gave it to her. They both then went up the court together.

I then went to the court to see if I could see them, but could not. I stood there for about three quarters of an hour to see if they came out, they did not, so I went away.

Hutchinson's description of the man himself goes into still further detail, specifying ethnicity as 'a foreigner'; height as 5ft 6in; age as 34 or 35; complexion as dark with a 'dark moustache turned up at the ends'; clothing as 'a long Astrakhan coat, a white collar with black necktie' complete with horseshoe pin; footwear as a 'pair of dark spats with light buttons over button boots'; and jewellery as including a watch chain, which had 'a big seal with a red stone hanging from it'. The description even extended to the man's dark eyelashes, absence of side whiskers and 'soft' manner of walking. Rounding off the description, Hutchinson mentioned:

The most detailed of the suspect descriptions was that given by George Hutchinson of a man he saw in the company of Mary Jane Kelly on the night of her death. (Mary Evans)

"HE TURNED AND LOOKED AT ME."

He carried a small parcel in his hand, about 8 inches long and it had a strap round it, he had it tightly grasped in his left hand, it looked as though it was covered in dark American cloth.

What is to be made of this remarkably detailed description? Hutchinson appears not to have been casually observing the couple so much as actively stalking them and eavesdropping on their conversation. Hutchinson was not called to give evidence at the one-day Kelly inquest and his evidence was thus never tested in public cross-examination. It is of course not impossible that individual recollection can be so detailed and precise, but the more obvious motive of attention-seeking in a high-profile murder case cannot be easily discounted. Certainly, given his close interest in Kelly, the fact that he was in the vicinity of Miller's Court close to the time of the murder, and that he was almost certainly the man spotted waiting outside the court by Sarah Lewis on the night of the murder, it is not surprising that in recent years Hutchinson has recently joined the list of what might be called 'sleeper suspects' – individuals who were apparently above suspicion at the time but whose role in the complex tapestry of the Ripper case has been reappraised and revisited by later historians of the case and armchair detectives, bringing them into the frame as suspects.

Mary Jane Kelly admits her killer to 13 Miller's Court. (Mary Evans)

Such were the five inquests on the Whitechapel Murders of 1888, each of them returning the same verdict of wilful murder against some person or persons unknown. It now fell to the men on the ground to attempt to put a face and a name to the anonymous killer.

# CHAPTER THREE: POLICING RIPPER STREET

## The Investigation

I have not been able to think of anything else for several days past [ . . . ] the idea has taken full possession of me, and everything fits in and dovetails so well that I cannot help feeling that this is the man we struggled so hard to capture fifteen years ago.

These were the impassioned words of retired Inspector Frederick George Abberline, one of the key detectives in the Ripper hunt, when reflecting on parallels between the case and another series of murders that had come to trial in 1903. What is striking in the inspector's words is less his belief that he had solved the case at last (he hadn't – the 1903 trial involved a poisoner with an entirely different MO) and more the sense of how deeply haunted he was by the events of 1888 and by the man who got away.

Other police officials looking back on the case took a more bluff stance. In his own reminiscences, Dr Robert Anderson, assistant commissioner of the Metropolitan CID at the time of the murders, implied that he in fact knew full well who the killer was:

I should almost be tempted to disclose the identity of the murderer [ . . . ] provided that the publishers would accept all responsibility in view of a possible libel action. But no public benefit would result from such a course, and the traditions of my old department would suffer.

One rather suspects the esteem and public standing of Anderson's 'old department' would be enhanced beyond measure had he successfully named the Ripper, but the bullishness of his stance reflects an understandable response to the years of criticism his force had endured for failing to lay hands on the perpetrator.

Anderson's equivalent number in the City of London force, Major Henry Smith, took this approach still further in his 1910 recollections of the case. Smith claimed not only that he knew more about the Whitechapel Murders case than any man living, but even that he had almost apprehended the killer, being 'within five minutes of him on one night, and with a very fair description of him besides'.

Clearly, in retrospect, many of the police officials involved with the Jack the Ripper investigation felt a need to rationalize or mitigate in their own minds the unsatisfactory outcome of the case. Their efforts to do so were kept alive by an interested press and public whose appetite for discussion of the murders, then as now, appeared insatiable. However, back in the autumn of 1888 as the series of murders unfolded, the police on the ground in 'Ripper Street' had no reason to suspect that these crimes would go unsolved and the murderer unpunished. They had a justifiable faith in the methodical nature of their policing, their detailed knowledge of the Ripper's killing ground, and their ability to reach the truth by means of vigilant, patient detective work.

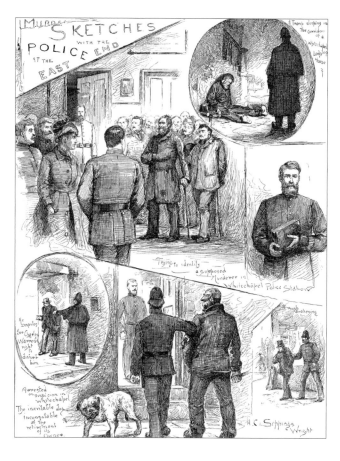

Policing Ripper Street: the interviews, searches, and arrests made during the course of the Ripper investigation. (Mary Evans)

## The Men on the Ground

At the time of the Ripper murders, the Metropolitan Police force had been in existence for almost 60 years. As the name implied, the force was responsible for policing the whole of the metropolis of London with the exception of the one square mile to the East known as the City of London, which, having been awarded a royal charter in the Middle Ages, had evolved its own force by the early 19th century, the City of London police force. The Ripper's 'double event' murders straddled the boundaries between the City and the Met; the subsequent sharing of information and collaboration between the two forces appears to have been relatively smooth, though at least one Ripperologist has suggested that the involvement of two separate forces in the Ripper case may equally have led to some confusions in the case and some curious inconsistencies in the historical record.

In 1888 the Metropolitan force was divided into 26 divisions covering the different London districts: the division responsible for the area of Whitechapel and Spitalfields was H Division. The Met's key men on the ground in the Whitechapel Murders case were as follows.

### Inspector Frederick George Abberline

At the time of the Ripper murders, Frederick George Abberline knew H Division and the killer's East End hunting grounds very well. He had been an inspector with the division for 14 years and had moved only the year before the murders to Scotland Yard, a promotion set in train by the chief constable of the Met's CID. Abberline was seconded back to Whitechapel when the murders began so that the investigation team might draw upon his expert knowledge of the East End streets and his pragmatic and efficient approach to detection. He worked under H Division boss Superintendent Thomas Arnold and alongside Inspector Edmund Reid, who had been appointed Abberline's successor as local inspector (head of CID) since his promotion to the Yard.

### Detective Constable Walter Dew

A detective constable in H Division at the time of the murders, Dew was later to become famous for his transatlantic pursuit of wife-murderer Dr Crippen, writing about the case in his 1938 memoirs, *I Caught Crippen*. Dew was closely involved in the Ripper investigation, conducting searches and interviews during the case and viewing, to his enduring discomfort, the remains of Mary Jane Kelly *in situ* in Miller's Court.

### Chief Inspector Donald Swanson

Swanson was chief inspector CID at the time of the Ripper murders and the man in charge of the case. He was not as voluble as some of his contemporaries in talking about the crimes in his retirement, though some marginal notes he wrote in his copy of a senior colleague's memoirs have featured prominently in some theories as to the Ripper's identity, and according to a report in *The Pall Mall Gazette* of 1895 Swanson was certain by that date that the Ripper was dead.

### Sergeant William Thick

An H Division officer who crops up repeatedly in the case is Sergeant William Thick, who arrested one of the earliest suspects in the case. Like Abberline, Thick knew the Ripper's hunting ground and the East End underworld very well, and was described by Walter Dew as 'a holy terror to the local law-breakers'.

These were the men at the forefront of the investigation. We have already met some of the cadre of police constables on the ground, patrolling the dark streets of Whitechapel with regulation issue whistles, bull lanterns, and truncheons. Together these officers formed the backbone of the Ripper enquiry, and were the men best placed either to catch the Ripper *in situ* or to run him to ground with methodical, dogged detective work.

# The Men in High Places

In contrast to the men on the ground, the policemen in high places often get a poor report in accounts of the Ripper case, being frequently characterized as at best complacent and at worst actively involved in collusion and conspiracy. Many of these unfavourable accounts simply reflect the disconnection that can arise between those at the sharp end of events and those seeking, in good faith but with less immediate and practical experience, to direct and guide events as best they can. There are three key figures we should consider.

## Sir Charles Warren

Probably the police official who fares worst in the posterity of the Ripper case, Sir Charles Warren was Metropolitan Police commissioner from 1886 to 1888, resigning on the day of the Mary Jane Kelly murder (though for reasons of internal politics rather than failure in the Whitechapel case).

A military man with broad interests who had served in Palestine, Warren viewed policing through the prism of military notions of strategy, discipline, and authority. At first, his hardline approach to policing appeared an appropriate response to the challenges of the day, which included growing civil and political

Sir Charles Warren. (Mary Evans)

unrest on the streets of London. But while skirmishes on Lord Mayor's Day 1886 and a Clerkenwell riot seemed to be contained effectively by his policing, the same methods proved inflammatory at the 'Bloody Sunday' riot in Trafalgar Square in November 1887. The accounts of the fracas in the radical press fixed perception of Warren as a stubborn hard-liner. Indeed, Sir Charles has even featured in a number of the conspiracy theories associated with the Ripper case – some of his less productive and supportive actions being reinterpreted as deliberately obstructive of attempts to uncover the truth about the Ripper.

## Dr Robert Anderson

Dr Robert Anderson, assistant commissioner of the Metropolitan Police CID, was demonstrably not 'on the ground' in the early phases of the Ripper enquiry. After taking up his post on the day of the Nichols murder, he promptly departed a week later for Switzerland on a month's sick leave, setting off on the day of the Chapman murder. It took the hysteria following the 'double event' to bring him back to London, where one of his recommendations for combating the crimes, if not detecting the killer, was to enforce a curfew on the streets of the East End and arrest all prostitutes who were abroad after midnight. Anderson's theory as to the identity of the Ripper was set out in some detail in the years following the case and will figure in the next chapter's review of suspects.

'Bloody Sunday', 13 November 1887. When Warren ordered the forceful dispersal of a mass demonstration of the unemployed in Trafalgar Square, the ensuing fracas led to many brutal injuries and one civilian death. The event alienated large sections of the public and press from the Metropolitan Police force and Warren became a hate figure in these quarters. (Mary Evans)

### Sir Melville MacNaughten

The last of the senior police officials to figure in the case came into post almost a year after the murders had ceased, but nevertheless went on to write more about the Ripper than any of his colleagues. Sir Melville MacNaughten (1853–1921) became assistant chief constable of the Metropolitan Police in 1889, later rising to chief constable and then assistant commissioner between 1903 and 1913. He would devote a chapter of his autobiography, *Days of My Years* (1914), to the Ripper case and would bequeath to posterity the vital documents now known as the 'MacNaughten Memoranda', which must feature in any discussion of Ripper suspects. While not 'on the ground' while the murders took place, MacNaughten appears to have sought out the facts doggedly after he came into post, and the facts he gathered and recorded in his memoranda lie at the heart of 'Ripperology' to this day.

## On the Scent

The methods employed for the detection and arrest of Jack the Ripper were varied, and some were more pragmatic than others. First, there was an increase in the physical presence of the police in uniform, plain clothes, and even, in some cases, in cross-dress. After the 'double event' murders of 29/30 September, this approach was extended to a policy of 'flooding' the East End with literally hundreds of men, drafting them from other London divisions. Detection methods included making systematic inquiries at the many East End lodging houses, distributing 80,000 leaflets to Whitechapel residents and making house-to-house enquiries within a fixed radius of the murder sites. The Thames Police made enquiries at the docks (the fact that the murders were occurring at weekends had prompted some suspicion that the Ripper was a sailor, out of town during the week). A report from Chief Inspector Swanson to the Home Secretary detailed how, as of 19 October 1888, approximately 80 individuals had been detained and interviewed by the police, detailed enquiries had been made into the movements and whereabouts at the time of the murders of some 300 citizens, and, within the specific occupational groups of butchers and slaughterers, 76 visits and detailed interviews had been conducted. Swanson's report carried an exasperated addendum from Sir Charles Warren, lamenting that all of these lines of enquiry had so far 'had no tangible result as far as the Whitechapel murders'.

## Off the Scent

As well as having to contend with the cunning and ingenuity of the genuine killer, the police also had to navigate the many false trails laid by hoaxers during the Ripper scare. Seminal Ripper author Donald Rumbelow relates how at the height of the autumn of terror, the police were receiving as many as a thousand letters a week claiming to be from the killer. The most famous of these letters had been sent in the first instance not to the police but to London's Central News Agency on 27 September 1888 from postal district EC1. Written in red ink, it was the letter that was to give the 'Whitechapel Murderer' a new name, the most famous in criminal history.

25 Sept 1888

Dear Boss,

I keep on hearing the police have caught me but they won't fix me just yet. I have laughed when they look so clever talk about being on the *right* track. That joke about Leather Apron gave me real fits. I am down on whores and I shan't quit ripping them till I do get buckled. Grand work the last job was. I gave the lady no time to squeal. How can they catch me now. I love my work and want to start again. You will soon hear of me with my funny little games. I saved some of the proper *red* stuff in a ginger beer bottle over the last job to write with but it went thick like glue and I cant use it. Red ink is fit enough I hope *ha. ha*. The next job I do I shall clip the ladys ears off and send to the police officers just for jolly wouldnt you. Keep this letter back till I do a bit more work, then give it out straight. My knife is nice and sharp I want to get to work right away if I get a chance. Good luck.

   Yours truly,

     Jack the Ripper

Don't mind me giving the trade name.

wasnt good enough to post this before I got all the red ink off my hands curse it.

No luck yet. They say I'm a doctor now *ha ha*.

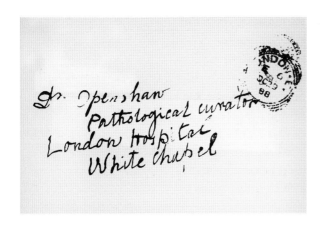

The follow-up letter to the 'Lusk kidney', sent to Dr Thomas Openshaw of the London Hospital in October 1888. (Mary Evans)

The letter was followed up on 1 October with a postcard written in an apparently identical hand and with a similarly goading tone:

> I was not codding dear old Boss when I gave you the tip, you'll hear about saucy Jacky's work tomorrow double event this time number one squealed a bit couldnt finish straight off. had not time to get ears for police thanks for keeping last letter back till I got to work again.
>
> Jack the Ripper

The letter and postcard created a sensation. The name 'Jack the Ripper' provided an immediate focus for the unease and anxiety in the East End: as we shall see, it moreover chimed with pre-existing images of bogeymen and folk-devils such as 'Spring Heeled Jack'. The arrival of the postcard so soon after the 'double event' murder and the apparent insider knowledge it contained meant that the epistles were taken very seriously. The Metropolitan Police published facsimiles of the documents, which were also transcribed in the press. Later opinion has generally viewed the communications as inspired hoaxes, Dr Robert Anderson viewing them as 'the creation of an enterprising London journalist', but their significance in the story of the Ripper as a cultural phenomenon cannot be overstated. They lie at the very heart of the textual web of the Ripper story.

There were two more 'Ripper' letters that were taken reasonably seriously by some quarters of the police. The first was sent to George Lusk, chairman of the Whitechapel Vigilance Committee, who received it on 16 October 1888, two weeks after the 'double event' murder.

> From hell
> Mr Lusk
> Sor
> I send you half the Kidne I took from one women prasarved it for you tother piece I fried and ate it was very nise. I may send you the bloody knif that took it out if you only wate a whil longer.
> signed
> Catch me when you can Mishter Lusk.

The tone and content of the letter are disturbing enough. The effect must have been magnified tenfold when Lusk found in the accompanying package half a human kidney. Lusk took the incident for a hoax, but the fact that the body of Mitre Square victim Catherine Eddowes was indeed missing the left kidney was sufficient basis for the grisly parcel to be turned over to the Pathology Museum of the London Hospital for examination. There the curator, Dr Thomas Openshaw, declared the kidney to be human – a point picked up and elaborated by the press, who seemed keen to consolidate the association with Eddowes. In the resulting publicity Dr Openshaw himself received a follow-up letter, almost certainly from a separate hoaxer. Postmarked 29 October, this one read:

> Old boss you was rite it was the left kidney I was goin to hoperate again close to your ospitle just as I was going to dror my nife along of er bloomin throte them cusses of coppers spoilt the game but I guess I wil be on the job soon and will send you another bit of innerds
>
> Jack the Ripper
>
> O have you seen the devle with his mikerscope and scalpel a-lookin at a kidney with a slide cocked up?

It is worth noting that while the police at the time gave measured and appropriate consideration to the 'Ripper letters', they were less inclined to be led astray by them than some modern 'Ripperologists'. As we shall see, some modern theories are too quick to assume that if they can link a particular letter with a particular suspect, they 'have their man'. Such a link, if it could ever be established, would prove their man to be a hoaxer, not a killer.

Perhaps the most audacious hoax, if it was intended as such, involved the dumping of a woman's torso in a highly symbolic spot – right under the policemen's noses in the foundations of the New Scotland Yard building, undergoing construction in autumn 1888 on the Embankment. The remains were found on 3 October 1888 in a spot that had been clear on 29 September, placing the event at the eye of the storm of hysteria that attended the 'double event' and the 'Dear Boss' correspondence. Police surgeon Thomas Bond was able to match the grisly finding to limbs that had recently been recovered from the Thames. The police suspected a medical student prank, but the press were quick to claim a Ripper connection and the incident made a further macabre contribution to the tapestry of hoaxes, copycats, and scares that surrounded the Whitechapel Murders.

## Copycats and False Alarms

The police also had copycat killings and false alarms to contend with. Though the murder of Mary Jane Kelly is now almost universally recognized as the last of the Ripper killings, four further murders down to 1891 kept the Ripper scare alive on the streets of the East End.

First there was the mysterious death of Rose Mylett, whose body was discovered in Clarke's Yard by Police Constable Robert Goulding in the early hours of 20 December 1888. There were no obvious signs of violence on

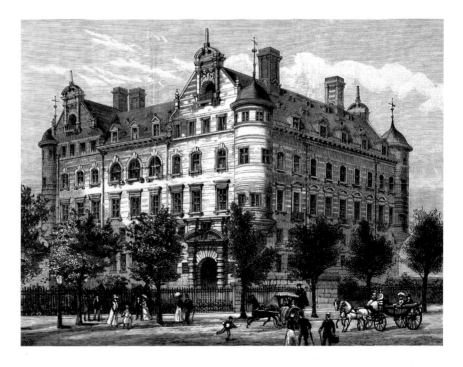

New Scotland Yard, the new headquarters of the Metropolitan Police, pictured in 1890. The mysterious appearance of a woman's torso in the foundations of the building in October 1888 made its own bizarre contribution to the Ripper maelstrom. (Mary Evans)

the body, though there was blood oozing from the nostrils and an abrasion to the right side of the face (both most likely caused when Rose fell to the ground). There was some speculation that this was a Ripper victim who had been strangled rather than despatched with a knife, and while foul play was widely suspected, post mortem evidence also raised the possibility of Rose having choked to death while drunk. Certainly, writing about the case in 1910, Sir Robert Anderson was confident that the case was one of 'death from natural causes, and but for the "Jack the Ripper" scare, no one would have thought of suggesting that it was a homicide'.

Next there was 'Claypipe Alice' McKenzie, whose body was discovered in Castle Alley by Police Constable Walter Andrews in the early hours of 17 July 1889. There were two knife wounds to her throat and a further two to her abdomen, which had been exposed, the clothing pulled up to the waist. Alice was identified by the clay pipe lying under her body. She was examined by two different doctors from the Ripper enquiry (Thomas Bond and George Bagster Phillips), who differed on whether she was a Ripper victim. Her inquest was conducted by Ripper coroner Wynne E. Baxter, who passed up the opportunity to speculate whether this was the Whitechapel killer at large again, instead drawing attention in his summing up to the wider picture of social deprivation and disadvantage that rendered women like 'Claypipe Alice' and so much of the East End population vulnerable:

> Here is a parish of 21,000 persons with only one church in it. There are not only cases of murder here, but many of starvation. I hope at least these cases

will open the eyes of those who are charitable to the necessity of doing their duty by trying to elevate the lower classes.

September 1889 saw another false alarm, many thinking a second 'autumn of terror' was in prospect, when on 10 September, Police Constable Pennett found a woman's torso under a railway arch in Pinchin Street. There was abdominal mutilation, and this was enough to spark off speculation in the press and on the streets, though the view of the police appears to have remained sceptical.

Finally, the body of Frances Coles or 'Carrotty Nell' was discovered in Swallow Gardens under some railway arches on 14 February 1891 by Police Constable Thompson of H Division. Frances was still alive but fading fast when Thompson found her, bleeding from a cut to her throat. As he knelt down to assist her, Thompson could hear footsteps, almost certainly those of her assailant, running away. Frances would pass away on the stretcher brought to the scene. Was she another Ripper victim? The police wanted to be sure one way or another, and thus no lesser persons than Robert Anderson and Melville MacNaughten visited the scene the next day with Chief Inspector Reid and Superintendent Robert Arnold of H Division. Suspicion soon fell not on the unknown serial killer who had been at large three years before but on James Thomas Sadler, a sailor who had known Frances well and publicly quarrelled with her on the day of her death. Though he would eventually escape trial for the crime, Sadler remained the prime suspect for the murder, a view confirmed in Melville MacNaughten's famous memoranda on the Ripper case.

A sketch of the body of 'Claypipe Alice' Mackenzie, whose murder in July 1889 prolonged the Ripper scare in the press. (Mary Evans)

## The Trail Goes Cold

From here, events moved swiftly to a close. Policing numbers in the East End were reduced and the civilian patrols of the Whitechapel Vigilance Committee also decreased, apparently on the basis of police intelligence that the Ripper threat had passed. There were to be no more shrill police whistles or paper boy cries of 'Orrible Murder' in the early hours. In 1892 the case was closed. The story of the Whitechapel Murders was at an end; the saga of unmasking 'Jack the Ripper' was just beginning.

# CHAPTER FOUR: SUSPECTS OF THE DAY

Who did the Victorian police suspect of being Jack the Ripper? Were they really no clearer as to his identity at the end of the series of crimes than at the start? Modern Ripper theories have widened the pool of suspects way beyond the small group of individuals given serious consideration at the time. These suspects were as few as five: one who was sought early in the series of murders, and four who emerged as suspects either during the killing spree or within a short time of its conclusion.

## Leather Apron

First there was 'Leather Apron'. As early as the murder of Mary Ann Nichols, the press reported that police were searching for a man who went by this nickname to assist them with their enquiries. He had been described to H Division police by a number of local prostitutes who claimed the man had threatened them, demanding money. Descriptions of the suspect varied, but the most prevalent description was of a short, burly man of about 38–40 with a thick neck, black hair, and black moustache. Elements of exaggeration and caricature seem to have crept into this description as it did the rounds. *The Star* newspaper of 6 September 1888 reported that 'A number of the street wanderers are in nightly terror of "Leather-Apron"', going on to give an evocative account of the police search for the suspect:

> The police are making efforts to arrest him, but he constantly changes his quarters. Some of the unfortunate women state that he is now in one of the low slums in the Borough. One of them said she saw him crossing London-bridge as stealthily as usual, with head bent, his skimpy coat turned up about his ears, and looking as if he were in a desperate hurry.
>
> The hunt for 'Leather Apron' began in earnest last evening. Constables 43 and 173, J Division, into whose hands 'Leather-Apron' fell on Sunday afternoon, were detailed to accompany Detective Enright, of the J Division, in a search through all the quarters where the crazy Jew was likely to be. They began at half-past ten in

(Mary Evans)

Church-street, in Shoreditch, rumor having located the suspected man there. They went through lodging-houses, into 'pubs', down side streets, threw their bull's-eyes into every shadow, and searched the quarter thoroughly, but without result.

There are some indications that 'Leather Apron' was not one man but many – a composite figure made up from various encounters between East End prostitutes and a selection of their more brutal, menacing, and intimidating clients. Indeed, some of the press accounts treat him almost as a mythical figure, a protopype for the Victorian bogeyman figure that 'Jack the Ripper' was to become.

Speculation about this suspect briefly intensified after the discovery of a leather apron by the corpse of Annie Chapman in Hanbury Street on 8 September (though it was to be dampened somewhat when the apron was claimed as the innocuous property of one of the Hanbury Street residents). However, 'Leather Apron' was to fade rapidly from the case after the appearance at the Chapman inquest of the man who apparently lay behind the alias, Polish Jewish leather worker John Pizer. Arrested on 10 September by Sergeant William Thick and summonsed to appear on Day 2 of the inquest, Pizer confirmed that he was indeed known as 'Leather Apron' and proceeded

**OVERLEAF:**
Did it all end here? The body of Montague John Druitt was retrieved from the Thames in Chiswick on New Year's Eve 1888.

39

M. J. Druitt

Montague John Druitt. (Mary Evans)

to give an account of his whereabouts on the murder nights. When Coroner Baxter confirmed to the jury 'it is only fair to say that the witness's statements can be corroborated', this first line of enquiry in the Ripper investigation appeared to have run its course and the name of 'Leather Apron' began to fade from the case. It would be all but forgotten after the name 'Jack the Ripper' displaced it in the public mind at the end of September 1888.[5]

## Suspects of the Day – The 'MacNaughten Memoranda'

Three of the four remaining Ripper suspects of the day are named by police official Sir Melville MacNaughten in the most famous, and arguably most significant, surviving documents relating to the Jack the Ripper case. Interestingly, the documents, known as the 'MacNaughten Memoranda', seem to have been produced not in the course of official record-keeping but in response to a speculative article in the popular press.

A piece in *The Sun* newspaper of 13 February 1894 had sought to indentify one Thomas Haines Cutbush as the Ripper. Having escaped from Lambeth Infirmary Asylum in March 1891, Cutbush carried out two separate knife assaults on women in Kennington. There were some suggestive aspects in Cutbush's profile, but these were not close enough to consolidate a connection with the Ripper, and MacNaughten, in going on record to say this, thought it also time that he set down his own insider view of the three most likely suspects to have been Jack the Ripper. In MacNaughten's order, these men were a Mr M. J. Druitt, a Polish Jew known as Aaron Kosminski, and a Russian doctor, Michael Ostrog.

### Montague John Druitt

Druitt was of the gentleman class. MacNaughten's notes describe him as a doctor, though he was in fact a schoolteacher with a legal training who was working at a boys' boarding school in Blackheath at the time of the Whitechapel Murders. Forty-one-year-old Druitt had studied at Winchester and Oxford, and played cricket with the Blackheath Cricket club. Beneath the respectable

---

5.  Ripper historians Paul Begg, Martin Fido, and Keith Skinner are characteristically astute in their observation that there remains confusion to this day as to who 'Leather Apron' really was and that this first line of enquiry would have been better renewed, not discarded, after Pizer was discounted as a suspect.

veneer, all was not well, however. For unknown reasons, Druitt was dismissed from his teaching post in November 1888, and, leaving suicide notes for his employer and family, he went missing shortly afterwards. The MacNaughten Memoranda place the disappearance at the time of the Miller's Court murder and relate how:

[his] body (which was said to have been upwards of a month in the water) was found in the Thames on 31 December – or about seven weeks after that murder. He was sexually insane and from private information I have little doubt but that his own family believed him to have been the murderer.

Druitt was clearly a serious suspect in MacNaughten's eyes, and while the retired police official felt by 1894 that the full truth would never be known, he remained of the view that it 'did indeed, at one time lie at the bottom of the Thames, if my conjections be correct'. It would be helpful to know more of the 'private information' to which MacNaughten was privy, for the case against Druitt seems to hinge largely on the circumstantial connection between the end of the murders and Druitt's suicide. Certainly, Inspector Abberline, interviewed in the *Pall Mall Gazette* in 1903, was unconvinced:

I know all about that story. But what does it amount to? Simply this. Soon after the last murder in Whitechapel the body of a young doctor was found in the Thames, but there is absolutely nothing beyond the fact that he was found at that time to incriminate him.

Despite subsequent attempts by researchers to assemble a more substantial case, the lack of incriminating evidence remains. The reason for Druitt's dismissal from the boys' school remains a mystery, but given MacNaughten's comment that he was 'sexually insane' (Victorian code for homosexual) it seems most likely that what lay behind the dismissal was not exposure as the East End murderer but an alleged or actual impropriety, leading to the schoolteacher's lonely suicide at the water's edge at the end of 1888. Yet neither has modern day research disproved the case against Montague John Druitt. When waterman Henry Winslade hauled up the body of a gentleman from the cold waters of the Thames at Chiswick, he may just have been recovering the body of Jack the Ripper.

### Aaron Kosminski

So many of the Victorian police views on the Ripper's identity diverge or conflict that it can be startling when they occasionally coincide. In the case of Aaron Kosminski, they do. Described by MacNaughten as a Polish Jew, resident in Whitechapel, who 'became insane owing to many years' indulgence in solitary vices', Kosminski is apparently also the 'low class' Jewish suspect

# GEORGE CHAPMAN

If true crime writer H. L. Adam, writing in 1930, is to be believed, there was one further Ripper suspect of the day, or at least shortly afterwards, in the eyes of Inspector Abberline. According to Adam's preface to *The Trial of George Chapman*, when wife-poisoner Chapman was arrested in 1902, Abberline reputedly told the arresting officer, 'You've got Jack the Ripper at last.' Whether the story is true or simply made a good addition to the marketing for Adam's book is moot. Researches into the Polish-born Chapman, whose original name was Severin Klosowski, reveal some suggestive details (he was resident in Whitechapel at the time of the murders and his employment as a barber gave him access to blades) but also some discouraging ones for consideration as the Ripper: he was younger than the man described in the most reliable of the Ripper witness statements, and he was at liberty until 1902 when he was arrested for murdering three successive women by means of poison (a markedly different MO from that of the Whitechapel Murderer). Chapman was hanged in 1903, taking any secrets he may have held regarding the Whitechapel Murders of 1888 with him to the grave.

described by Dr Robert Anderson in his own recollections of the case, *The Lighter Side of My Official Life* (1910) – a coincidence clinched when Chief Inspector Donald Swanson wrote on the margins of his copy of Anderson's book 'Kosminski was the suspect'.

On the basis of the surviving Ripper documents, then, Kosminski is by far the man most likely to have been the Ripper. He also fits the most likely profile of the killer, living locally to the murder sites, being of the same class as the victims (thus more likely to blend in than a gentleman), and with an apparent hatred of women and prostitutes in particular.

If only the historical record were equally obliging. The extensive research that has been conducted into Kosminski has turned up a series of paradoxes and dead ends. Aaron Kosminski, born around 1864, was only admitted to an asylum a full two years after the last Ripper murder and lived on in Colney

Colney Hatch Lunatic Asylum where Aaron Kosminski passed his last days, dying in 1919. Puzzlingly, the date of his death does not tally with Chief Inspector Swanson's assertion that the prime suspect in the case (whom he names as Kosminski) died shortly after he was incarcerated in Colney Hatch. The contradiction undermines the otherwise promising case against this Ripper suspect. (Mary Evans)

**PREVIOUS PAGE:**
How a contemporary line-up of key Ripper suspects might have looked: (from left to right) Polish Jewish immigrant Aaron Kosminski; schoolmaster and cricketer Montagu John Druitt; the American 'quack' doctor Francis Tumblety; and H Division's original suspect 'Leather Apron'.

Hatch Asylum until 1919, long after police officials were confidently asserting that the 'Polish Jew' Ripper suspect was dead.

Moreover, the few surviving medical records that document his time in the asylum do not reflect the kind of profound psychological disturbance that the Ripper must have experienced. Outside the writings of MacNaughten, Anderson, and Swanson, the case against Kosminski appears to collapse.[6] Abberline, again in *The Pall Mall Gazette*, was quick to dismiss it:

> I know [ ... ] that it has been stated in certain quarters that 'Jack the Ripper' was a man who died in a lunatic asylum a few years ago, but there is nothing at all of a tangible nature to support such a theory.

### Michael Ostrog

The third suspect named in the MacNaughten Memoranda was:

> MICHAEL OSTROG, a mad Russian doctor and a convict and unquestionably a homicidal maniac. This man was said to have been habitually cruel to women, and for a long time was known to have carried about surgical knives and other instruments; his antecedents were of the very worst and his whereabouts at the time of the Whitechapel murders could never be satisfactorily accounted for. He is still alive.

Latter day researches into Ostrog reveal a confidence trickster, born around 1833, and a man who employed a string of aliases and had many run-ins with with the law in locations as widely spread as Oxford, Cambridge, Maidstone, and Burton-on-Trent. Between September 1887 and March 1888 he had been incarcerated in the Surrey Pauper Lunatic Asylum. His discharge in the spring of 1888 apparently put him at liberty during the Ripper scare, and shortly after the 'double event' the Police Gazette published a wanted notice for 'this dangerous man'. But by the 1890s his appearances in the criminal records are for petty thefts rather than serial murder, and he disappears from the historical record completely after entering a Christian mission in Holborn in 1904.

Recent research suggests that Ostrog, again using an alias, was in a French prison during the time of the Ripper murders. Moreover, he deviates in key respects from what subsequent knowledge of serial murder tells us about the likely profile of Jack the Ripper. The fact that he enjoyed sporadic periods of liberty long after the murders had stopped is problematic for Ostrog's candidacy as the Ripper. The likelihood of a serial killer de-escalating his

---

6. The contribution made by the writers who have researched and set out the case for Kosminski should not, however, be underestimated. Their emphasis on the historical and written record of the case has demonstrably elevated the quest of 'hunt the Ripper' from parlour game to serious historical endeavour.

crimes to petty theft after the 'autumn of terror' is vanishingly small. MacNaughten himself suggested:

> A much more rational theory is that the murderer's brain gave way altogether after his awful glut in Miller's Court, and that he immediately comitted suicide, or, as a possible alternative, was found to be so hopelessly mad by his relations, that he was by them confined in some asylum.

## Francis Tumblety

A 1913 letter from a police official to the journalist G. R. Sims puts one further original Ripper suspect in the frame, this one a doctor. In 1888 Inspector John George Littlechild was head of Special Branch, a post he would retain until his retirement in 1893. It seems that the intelligence network Littlechild put in place to detect and prevent Fenian terrorist outrages in the capital (like the dynamite attack on the Old Scotland Yard building in 1884) brought to his notice the furtive East End activities of American doctor Francis Tumblety:

June 1884: Londoners contemplate damage caused by Fenian terrorists' dynamite attack on Scotland Yard. The intelligence network set up to monitor and avert such activities apparently alerted Inspector John George Littlechild to one Francis Tumblety, a Ripper suspect who would otherwise be lost to history. (Mary Evans)

> [A]mongst the suspects, and to my mind a very likely one, was a Dr T. (which sounds much like D.) He was an American quack named Tumblety and was

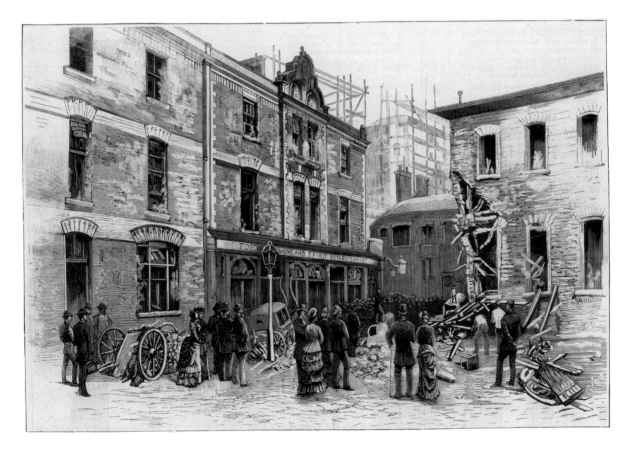

at one time a frequent visitor to London and on these occasions constantly brought under the notice of police, there being a large dossier concerning him at Scotland Yard. Although a 'Sycopathia Sexualis' subject he was not known as a 'Sadist' (which the murderer unquestionably was) but his feelings toward women were remarkable and bitter in the extreme, a fact on record. Tumblety was arrested at the time of the murders in connection with unnatural offences and charged at Marlborough Street, remanded on bail, jumped his bail, and got away to Boulogne. He shortly left Boulogne and was never heard of afterwards. It was believed he committed suicide but certain it is that from this time the 'Ripper' murders came to an end.

When the 'Littlechild letter' was rediscovered in 1993, the long forgotten suspect re-entered the frame, several aspects of his profile chiming suggestively with that of the killer: he had a documented hatred of women; he collected anatomical specimens; he was in London at the right time and was arrested and questioned at the height of the Ripper scare; he left London at the time the murders ceased.

Against these points, however, can be set the facts that Tumblety preferred the company of male prostitutes; that his rather dubious branch of medicine merely involved administration of 'quack' herbal remedies requiring little anatomical knowledge;  and that he lived on at liberty until 1903 after his return to America.

Our knowledge of 'Ripper suspects of the day' is still growing. The events of 125 years ago are still not so very remote: new documents and information still come to light, such as the 'Littlechild letter' naming previously unknown suspect Tumblety. If such new finds generally deepen the mystery rather than resolve it, they nevertheless help us to distinguish the genuine Ripper suspects of the day from the welter of suspects that have been suggested since. So legion in number are these suspects, they require a chapter of their own.

# CHAPTER FIVE: SUSPECTS OF TODAY

Everyone enjoys a good 'whodunnit' – a genre where the rules are comfortingly familiar. Act One introduces the first crime and initial clues; the middle acts provide suspects, settings, red herrings, and follow-up crimes; and, crucially, the final act provides answers, unmasking the killer and tying up loose ends. The Ripper story lacks this final act and the reassuring sense of closure that accompanies it. Our curiosity and our frustration with the open-ended nature of the story make us want to pick up where the Victorian police left off and hunt the Ripper ourselves.

It is probably no accident that the first post-Victorian attempts to solve the Ripper crimes coincided with the Golden Age of detective fiction. This period in the 1920s and 30s saw Agatha Christie's Poirot, Dorothy L. Sayers' Lord Peter Wimsey, and Ngaio Marsh's Inspector Alleyn at work investigating crimes between the covers of inexpensive paperback novels, greedily consumed by a middle class readership (it was also the period in which Sir Arthur Conan Doyle wrote the last of his Sherlock Holmes stories). Contemplating crime from the comfort of one's armchair had become a respectable and even light-hearted pursuit.

Since that time, a welter of suspects has been added to the Jack the Ripper hall of infamy. It is increasingly a challenge to consider them all, but it is still possible to group the majority into four key camps. First, there are 'Gentleman Jack' suspects, where a Victorian professional of good standing – often a doctor – maintains an image of respectability by day, transforming by night into the dreaded Ripper; second, there are 'Great Victorians', where a figure known to posterity as

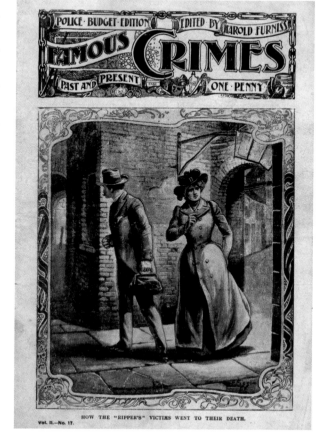

The classic image of the killer as 'Gentleman Jack', complete with hat and Gladstone bag. (Mary Evans Picture Library / Alamy)

one of the great or good of Victorian society is 'unmasked' as the dreaded Ripper, their guilt perhaps having been covered up at the time by men in high places; from there it is a short step to conspiracy theories, which took off in earnest after the US Watergate scandal of the 1970s; and finally, there is the modern vogue for 'sleeper suspects' – apparently minor characters in the Ripper saga such as mortuary attendants, market porters, and witnesses, whose names have been in the historical record since the start of the case and who are now revisited, one by one, as potential Ripper suspects.

## 'Gentleman Jack' Suspects

Leonard Matters' book on the Whitechapel Murders, *The Mystery of Jack the Ripper*, appeared before the reading public in 1929. The first full-length study of the case, the book recognized that the Ripper murders were ripe for revisiting given 'the demand that exists for detective novels' and that 'the murders were the sensation of that age; the sensation of the world'. Matters' book honours the conventions of the detective novel by not simply exploring the mystery of the Ripper but seeking to solve it. A suspect is duly provided: Matters' Ripper was 'Dr Stanley', a distinguished medic who had practised at Charing Cross Hospital, whose son had contracted syphilis from an East End prostitute and died in shame.

> What if this lad – the son of such a father – died a fatal wreck as the consequence of some worthless woman's fatal fascination for him? Would it turn the saturnine Dr Stanley into the satanic instrument of vengeance upon that woman? Would it make this surgeon 'Jack the Ripper'? It would, and it did.
>
> (*The Mystery of Jack the Ripper*, Chapter 21)

Psychic medium Robert James Lees who allegedly followed the psychic trail of the Ripper to the front door of a respectable London doctor. (Mary Evans Picture Library / Alamy)

Thus transformed from respectable Jekyll to vengeful Hyde, Matters' 'Dr Stanley' went on a murderous spree through the East End as he gradually and inevitably tracked down the woman who had been the undoing of his son and of his hopes – one Mary Jane Kelly.

While 'Dr Stanley' remains an utterly mysterious figure (who may have escaped to Buenos Aires after the murders but equally may never have existed), Matters' view of a 'Gentleman Jack' Ripper, or, as he put it, 'a veritable case of "Dr Jekyll and Mr Hyde"', has been perpetuated in theories ever since.

It is also clear that Matters was picking up and retelling an *existing* Ripper theory when he wrote his book in 1929, rather than inventing it afresh. Proof of this comes from an article in *The Chicago Sunday Times Herald* of April 1895, which described how the spiritualist medium Robert James Lees had apparently experienced a psychic vision of the Ripper at the height of the murder scare, shortly afterwards seeing the same man in the flesh boarding a London omnibus. The story's climax reveals how shortly afterwards, Lees, in the company of the police, followed the psychic trail of the Ripper to the West End home of an eminent London physician who, when revealed to be the killer, was incarcerated in an asylum. Scandal was averted by faking the good doctor's death and holding a sham funeral.

Sir William Withey Gull (1816–90). Was he the doctor traced by psychic Robert James Lees as the potential Ripper? (Mary Evans)

While the reliability of this story has been much questioned over the years, it was revived to dramatic effect in 1970 when Dr Thomas Stowell weighed into the case by publishing an article entitled 'Jack the Ripper – A Solution?' in *The Criminologist*. Stowell speculated that the doctor who received the nocturnal visit from Lees and the police at the height of the murders was no less than royal physician Sir William Gull. A more eminent 'Gentleman Jack' one could hardly ask for – Gull was Physician in Ordinary to Queen Victoria herself and closely associated with the royal household. Stowell's speculation arose after he learned from Gull's daughter, Caroline Acland, that when she was a child, their household had received a night-time visit at the height of the murders from a police officer and a man calling himself a medium. Questioned by the visitors, Gull had admitted to memory lapses since suffering a slight stroke in 1887. He further mentioned that he had recently awoken to find blood on his shirt after just such a blackout.[7]

While nothing has ever been found to verify this story drawn from Stowell's reminiscences, Gull's name has faded in and out of the Ripper case ever since.

7. Suprisingly, Stowell takes the bloodstained shirt to incriminate not Gull himself but, as we shall see below, one of his royal patients.

## JILL THE RIPPER

It is somewhat surprising in retrospect that Sir Arthur Conan Doyle, creator of legendary Victorian detective Sherlock Holmes, did not have more to say about the Ripper case. The first Holmes story, *A Study in Scarlet*, appeared in 1887, the year before the Ripper murders, and throughout his lifetime Doyle was known for involving himself in cases of true crime, often taking up the causes of wrongfully accused suspects.

The little Doyle apparently did say about the Ripper addressed the thorny issue of how the killer was able to pass through the streets of Whitechapel unnoticed when at least some of his crimes must have left him spattered with blood. Doyle's solution was to suggest the police look for not Jack but Jill the Ripper. Perhaps the murderer was cross-dressing in the guise of a midwife, or perhaps the killer was indeed a woman. The notion was taken up by William Stewart in his 1939 book on the case, *Jack the Ripper: A New Theory*, which suggested that 'Jill the Ripper' may have been a backstreet abortionist and that the Ripper murders were in fact the result of her botched operations. As a candidate for Jill, Stewart suggested Victorian murderess Mary Pearcey (who was hanged in 1890 for the murder of a mother and child). The theory resurfaces sporadically to this day.

Just as Robert James Lees seems to have been haunted until his dying days by his vision of the Ripper, so the image of 'Dr Jekyll at the court of Queen Victoria' has simply proved too vivid and enduring for Ripperology to shake off.

### James Maybrick

Gentleman Jack need not have been a doctor. What if he was a successful business man? Prior to his name entering the Ripper investigation in 1993, James Maybrick had been known to history as a victim rather than a perpetrator of crime. The Liverpool-based cotton merchant had been the victim of a notorious murder case of 1889, apparently suffering death by strychnine poisoning at the hands of his wife Florence.

Florence's high-profile trial at St George's Hall, Liverpool had commanded widespread coverage in the press, and indeed headlines from the 1889 trial appeared alongside accounts of the Ripper-style murders that were still taking place in Whitechapel, challenging posterity to link the two cases. Someone did link them in 1992, when a manuscript of very uncertain provenance was put forward as the putative 'Diary of Jack the Ripper'. Purportedly the diary of James Maybrick (though the author is nowhere named), the diarist claims responsibility for the Whitechapel Murders and suggests that the unfortunate victims were suffering vicarious punishment for Florence's infidelities.

The appearance of a 'Jack the Ripper diary' was always likely to cause a splash. Arriving a decade after the notorious 'Hitler diaries', a hoax that had damaged the credibility of much expert opinion, the controversy over the 'Ripper diary' was focused less on the question of 'is it a fake?' and more upon 'when was it faked and by whom?' The subsequent confessions of forgery that have emerged, plus the fact that there is nothing in the diary that could not have been gleaned from the published literature on Jack the Ripper, mean that the 'Ripper diary' should be seen as just another eccentric entry in the 'Gentleman Jack' tradition of suspects – a tradition that looks likely to continue as long as interest in the case lasts.

Liverpool cotton merchant James Maybrick. (Mary Evans)

## 'Great Victorian' Suspects

Most of the 'Great Victorian' suspects in the Ripper case are only half-seriously suggested, making for good headlines in the popular press but rarely supported by a shred of evidence. Such theories have often arisen when, in curious coincidences of history, eminent Victorians have played small cameo roles in the case. These short walk-on parts have been seized upon and magnified by later theorists claiming, often mischievously, a greater significance for them than has previously been suggested. Thus a chance comment in Lewis Carroll's 1888 diary, recording that he has chatted about the murders to a friend, is seized upon to name the author of *Alice in Wonderland* as Jack the Ripper, while the chance meeting of a Ripper victim and a great Victorian philanthropist during one of his charitable visits to the East End in 1888 has also brought his name into the frame. The greatest of the 'Great Victorians' to receive this treatment is even of royal blood. Let us consider three such 'Great Victorians'.

### Dr Barnardo

Committed philanthropist Thomas Barnardo (1845–1905) arguably deserved better than to be accused by posterity of being Jack the Ripper. His Victorian work for the poor and destitute, born out of a strong sense of Christian mission, still exerts a legacy to this day. Barnardo was particularly concerned with making adequate food and housing provision for the children of the East End, and to this purpose 1888 found him visiting the dosshouses of Whitechapel on a campaign to convince prostitutes to entrust his charity with the care of their children so that they might be provided for more reliably. Among the dosshouses visited by Barnardo was 32 Flower and Dean Street, where he spent some time talking to a group of women in the kitchen, the topics of conversation including the Ripper scare. He wrote to *The Times* newspaper recounting the haunting words of one of them:

> I found the women and girls thoroughly frightened by the recent murders, one poor creature, who had apparently been drinking, cried bitterly, 'We're all up to no good and no one cares what becomes of us, perhaps some of us will be killed next'.

The words proved to be prophetic, for among the group huddled around the kitchen table that day was the fourth Ripper victim, Elizabeth Stride – an identification confirmed by Barnardo himself when he later viewed her body at the mortuary.

Kept in proportion, the incident is one of those curious intersections of history that can bring the past vividly to life, but it is unlikely to be anything more. While there may well have been some suspicion surrounding doctors visiting dosshouses during the murders, there is no indication of serious police suspicion of Barnardo at the time and, more likely, the suggestion of Barnardo as a suspect is simply another twist on the 'Gentleman Jack' image of the Ripper, with the added frisson that his celebrity and posterity bring.

## J. K. Stephen

Less of a 'Great Victorian' in his own right, but certainly moving in the circles of the great and the good, was Cambridge academic and poet James Kenneth Stephen. First suggested as a Ripper suspect in a 1972 book by Michael Harrison, Stephen was the son of Sir Leslie Fitzjames Stephen, the eminent judge who had presided at the trial of Florence Maybrick, and cousin to the novelist Virginia Woolf. Born in 1859, Stephen was juggling a portfolio career as writer, poet, Cambridge scholar, and lawyer when he suffered a blow to the head in an accident in 1886.

Personality change, depression, and eventual death in 1892 followed. Harrison suggested that during the period of his decline Stephen might have developed homicidal tendencies, pointing as evidence to some apparently

James Kenneth Stephen, variously proposed as suspect and accomplice in different Ripper theories.
(Mary Evans)

misogynistic verse amongst his writings, and to some apparent similarities between Stephen's handwriting and the 'From Hell' and 'Old Boss' Ripper letters. The case against him is paper thin, lacking even circumstantial evidence. It nevertheless made a splash in the press in the early 1970s, not so much on account of Stephen himself but because of the company he kept. For the book naming Stephen as a suspect was a biography of a still greater Victorian – a member of Stephen's Cambridge cohort, Prince Albert Victor, Duke of Clarence and Avondale – who also has been suggested as Jack the Ripper.

## Prince Albert Victor, or 'Eddy'

The idea that the Whitechapel Murders might have been perpetrated by a member of the Victorian royal family is among the most outlandish theories regarding the identity of Jack the Ripper. It has never been seriously entertained, but it has always made a good story. The story first emerged in 1970, when the aforementioned Dr Thomas Stowell published his article 'Jack the Ripper – A Solution?' in *The Criminologist*. The article suggested that a high-ranking individual, described only as 'S' for 'suspect', was responsible for the Whitechapel Murders. The crimes were enacted during fits of mania, the young gentleman having contracted syphilis from a prostitute and having developed a lust for human blood and mutilation after many years' participation in bloodsports:

> 'S' was scion of a noble house, the heir to an illustrious title and great wealth. He was under medium height and had a fair moustache and wore a deer stalker hat in which to commit his acts of raving lunacy.

Learning with horror of his crimes, this high-ranking gentleman's family enlisted the help of their physician to avert further murders. He was thus admitted to a private mental hospital shortly after the 'double event' murders in Berner Street and Mitre Square. Nevertheless he escaped to kill one last time, and thus did Mary Jane Kelly fall victim to him in the last nightmarish Ripper killing. Recaptured, he was incarcerated until his death in 1892 from 'softening of the brain' caused by syphilis, though his family communicated the official cause as influenza, a flu epidemic having swept the British Isles that year.

For all its coded reference to 'S' and its guarded approach, the inference of Stowell's article was clear. The finger of accusation was being pointed at the Victorian royal household, and the candidate being so audaciously suggested as Jack the Ripper was Queen Victoria's grandson, Prince Albert Victor, known familiarly as 'Eddy' – who in 1888 was second in line to the throne.

The 'Royal Ripper' story caused an international sensation and endured for at least a decade – the 1978 book by Frank Spiering, *Prince Jack*, broadening the pool of conspirators involved in the cover-up and the 1997 film *The Ripper* reviving the notion of 'Eddy' as the killer. Away from the sensationalist headlines, however, the 'Royal Ripper' theory was quickly debunked. Examination of court records and other official documents by Clarence's biographer Michael Harrison quickly established that the prince was not only elsewhere at the times of the murders, but often as far afield as the royal estates at Sandringham and Balmoral. Compelling as the theory of 'Prince Jack' may be, the only genuine connection between the royal family and the Jack the Ripper murders is the concerned comments Queen Victoria is on record as having made at the time:

> This new most ghastly murder shows the absolute necessity for some very decided action. All these courts must be lit, and our detectives improved.

## Conspiracy Theories

'There can be no whitewash in the White House,' averred President Nixon at the height of the 1973 Watergate scandal, but had there been one in

# WALTER SICKERT

One legacy of the conspiracy Ripper theory is the continued suggestion that painter Walter Sickert (1860–1942) might have been the Ripper. Unlike many of the other suspects whose names have been drawn into the world of 'armchair Ripperology', Sickert would probably have been somewhat taken with the suggestion: he is known to have had a deep interest in the Ripper case, painted a work entitled 'Jack the Ripper's Bedroom', and, according to some contemporary accounts by friends and associates, would even walk the streets of the East End by night dressed in the stereotypical image of the Ripper.

Jean Overton Fuller's *Sickert and the Ripper Crimes* (1990; revised 2003) sought to explore whether there was anything more than eccentric behaviour behind Sickert's fixation, while crime fiction writer Patricia Cornwell has devoted considerable funds, time, and energy to attempting to link the artist with original 'Ripper letters' by controversially harvesting DNA from one of his paintings and even his old writing desk.

Eccentric English painter Walter Sickert. (Mary Evans)

Whitechapel? Author Stephen Knight thought so and in 1975 set out to prove it with the publication of the hugely influential *Jack the Ripper: The Final Solution*. Knight's theory drew together some of the most sensational elements of preceding theories – a royal connection, the psychic medium, and the doctor gone wrong – linking them in an elaborate conspiracy theory. The story was as follows: in 1885 Prince Albert Victor had contracted a clandestine marriage and fathered a child with a young woman by the name of Annie Crook, whom he had met when visiting the Cleveland Street studio of the painter Walter Sickert. Annie was neither of noble birth nor of Anglican denomination, insuperable obstacles to securing royal approval for the match. The tryst was discovered by Eddy's horrified family, who feared an anti-monarchist uprising if the scandal were to break. Henchmen were sent to seize the couple and separate them in a raid on Cleveland Street.

The prince was kept under close watch and Annie was lobotomized and committed to an asylum. But the scandal could not be contained so easily: the couple's infant daughter, Alice, had escaped the raid, safe in the arms of her nurse – one Mary Jane Kelly, who smuggled her to safety. Mary, now forced to eke out a living by prostitution in the East End, shared her

**OPPOSITE:**
In the central icon of the Masonic Ripper conspiracy theory, a sinister closed carriage rolls through the East End, the driver keeping the horses at a steady trot while the carriage's occupant scours the streets for the next victim.

A depiction of a Freemason initiation ceremony in the 1890s. Ripper conspiracy theories have suggested that the wounds sustained by Jack the Ripper's victims can be explained by references elsewhere in Masonic tradition to punishment by disembowelling. (Mary Evans)

knowledge of the scandal with four of her companions. When they attempted to use what they knew to blackmail the highest in the land, the Ripper murders began – not the work of a lone lunatic but the calculating elimination of witnesses by a conspiracy of three men: coach driver John Netley, royal physician Sir William Gull and the man who would recognize Mary Jane Kelly on sight, Walter Richard Sickert. While all London was looking out for a sinister lone figure prowling the streets of Whitechapel, the real killers were rattling through the streets in a closed carriage stalking the victims in turn. Lured into the apparent safety of the carriage, the victims would be drugged and then horrifically mutilated by Gull. The mutilations themselves had a significance in this theory: the opening of the abdomen and extraction of the intestines would, Knight claimed, be recognized as holding ritual significance for anyone familiar with the customs and traditions of Freemasonry. The mutilations, it was suggested, thus sent a signal to other Freemasons – including those high up in the police and detective forces – to hold back from certain lines of enquiry.

Much like the preceding story of 'Prince Jack', the Ripper conspiracy theory had more of sensation than sense about it. According to Knight, the Masonic conspiracy extended to embrace Prime Minister Lord Salisbury, Dr Robert Anderson, and Sir Charles Warren of the Metropolitan Police, and many more. Meanwhile, the informant from whom the whole story had derived retracted the tale within a year of Knight's book appearing. Yet the theory has been profoundly influential and has shaped all of the major film portrayals of the Ripper story for the last 40 years. Just as the Jekyll and Hyde picture of the Ripper seemed to provide the perfect image for late Victorian anxieties and preoccupations, so the notion of the Ripper-conspirator fits tellingly with the fears of our own age.

## Modern Theories: 'Sleeper Suspects'

The majority of Ripper theories over the last two decades have hinged not on introducing completely new suspects into the case, but on reshuffling the existing cast of characters in the Ripper story and reassessing them in turn as potential suspects. What if we have in fact had the name of the Ripper before us in the files all along? Might he be hiding in plain sight? Could he be the witness at an inquest whose testimony we previously took in good faith? Might one of the men who 'found' the bodies in fact have been the killer himself, raising the alarm and revelling in misleading the authorities? Suspects such as these might be called 'sleeper suspects' – individuals who have been in the case all along but whose significance we have not fully grasped.

An 1888 edition of the *Illustrated Police News*. Is the killer still 'hiding in plain sight' in records such as these? Most modern Ripper theories assume that the real killer is someone already known to us from the files. Was he the mortuary attendant who ferried the victim's bodies away from the crime scenes? Was he the lodging house keeper who was among the last to see Annie Chapman alive? Was he the night watchman in Mitre Square whose door on the night of the double murder was left ajar? So steeped are we in the conventions of the fictional 'whodunnit' that the urge to join the hunt for the Ripper from amongst these 'sleeper suspects' is almost overwhelming. (Lordprice Collection / Alamy)

Thus for writer Bruce Paley in *Jack the Ripper: The Simple Truth* (1996) the killer is Mary Jane Kelly's on-off partner Joe Barnett. For M. J. Trow, writing in *Jack the Ripper: Quest for a Killer* (2009), it is mortuary attendant Robert Mann, his apparent hapless washing of the body of Mary Ann Nichols being in fact a deliberate destruction of evidence. For other writers, the detailed description given by George Hutchinson of the man he saw with Mary Jane Kelly was all a smokescreen – Hutchinson himself was the Ripper. More recently, yet another 'sleeper suspect' has awoken. This time it is market porter Charles Cross, the man who 'discovered' the body of first Ripper victim Polly Nichols.

The dominant notion in modern Ripper theories seems to be that we have a closed pool of suspects named within the existing literature. It is tempting to wonder how far this approach to Ripperology has been cross-fertilized by the conventions of crime fiction, the rules of which dictate that the murderer, when finally revealed, is never a completely new character but someone already known to us. Just as the sleuth proclaims at the denouement of many a detective novel that 'the killer is in this very room', so the 'sleeper suspect' approach to the Ripper case suggests that somewhere in the files and literature lies the solution to the 125-year-old mystery. It is an approach that may yet prove correct. But with a cast of characters as extensive as that which features in the Ripper story, the long process of elimination may take a good while yet.

Looking back on the major Ripper suspects to have emerged since 1970, it is clear that to some extent the individuals put forward as Ripper candidates have reflected the preoccupations of their age. Thus the 'Royal Ripper' theory made its international splash in 1970, hard on the heels of 1960s questioning of established authority and at the start of a decade that would find the Sex Pistols singing an ironic 'God Save the Queen' in their single *Anarchy in the UK*. Likewise the Ripper conspiracy theory would make its full global impact shortly after the US Watergate scandal had demonstrated just how audacious and extensive an organized cover up by 'men in high places' could be. Finally, the 'sleeper suspects' tradition we have witnessed since 1988 reflects not just genuine advances in serial killer psychological profiling and forensic science but also the popularity of these themes in film and television, from *The Silence of the Lambs* (1990) to *CSI: Crime Scene Investigation* (2000–present). If the original image of 'Gentleman Jack' has endured because it captures key Victorian ideas (and anxieties) concerning class, sexuality, and psychology, it seems likely that these later images of the Ripper tell us something of the preoccupations and fixations of our own times.

# CHAPTER SIX: JACK IN THE BOOKS
## The Ripper as Dramatis Persona

Mention Jack the Ripper or Sherlock Holmes and you evoke the same response. Images crowd the mind of fog, hansom cabs, gas-lit cockney pubs, crumpets for tea, top hats, red silks, scarlet women and romance for a guinea – with change at the end of the evening! It is a totally fictitious world.

(Donald Rumbelow's Preface to the first edition of Paul Begg, Martin Fido, and Keith Skinner's *Jack the Ripper A to Z*).

When did Jack the Ripper become a *dramatis persona*, a character from a fictional world rather than a real one? At what point did the brutal reality of his crimes become overshadowed by a more theatrical and caricatured set of images and associations? The answer seems to be – from the start. Even as the events of autumn 1888 were still unfolding, so the press and the public were embellishing the facts and mixing them with elements from fiction, legend, and literature.

First, there were the press accounts, sensational in tone and always ready to elaborate upon the facts surrounding the Whitechapel Murders, adding additional intrigue and speculation. Then, there were 'Jack's forebears' – pre-existing bogeyman from folktale and legend with which the figure of the Ripper seems to have been merged at an early stage. Finally, there was a group of late Victorian novels that drew the figure of the Ripper into a textual web of Gothic anti-heroes and stage villains.

## Press Accounts of the Ripper Scare

The press accounts of the Ripper scare played a key role in ensuring the notoriety of the Whitechapel Murders. Some of the press coverage was rightly motivated by a sense of the injustice of the squalor of the East End relative to the opulence of the West, and the appalling vulnerability of the women who were falling victim to the Ripper's knife. But by far the majority of the accounts were melodramatic and sensational. The popular press learned early

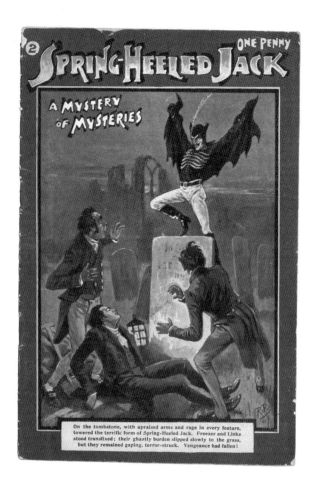

Spring Heeled Jack would appear suddenly, inciting panic in those he accosted and, after terrorizing them, would vanish apparently into thin air as suddenly as he had appeared. This figure from folktale clearly provided a blueprint for some of the most abiding aspects of the figure of the Ripper. (Mary Evans)

in the series of murders that the Ripper sold papers in significant numbers. There was good cause not only to recount the details of the murders but to speculate on the murderer's identity and to propose theories as to how he escaped detection. The impact these accounts could have on Victorian readers is perhaps best demonstrated by an article from *The Star* of 13 September 1888:

Mrs Mary Burridge, a dealer in floor-cloth, at 132, Blackfriars-road, was standing at her door on Saturday, reading the *Star* account of the Whitechapel murder, and was so much affected that she retired to the kitchen, where she fell down in a fit. She regained consciousness for a short time on Monday, but afterwards relapsed and died yesterday.

As poor Mrs Burridge's extreme reaction implies, many of the lurid press accounts of the murders courted a visceral response, drawing freely on images and motifs from Gothic literature and the sensation novel. The Ripper 'comes as unseen and vanishes as quickly as Frankenstein's monster,' said an edition of *The Glasgow Herald* that autumn; the Ripper was 'a ghoul like creature who stalks through the streets of London … simply drunk with blood – and he will have more,' said *The Star* of 8 September; while according to the *East London Advertiser* of the same date, the killer was 'like another Hyde'.

In doing this, the newspaper accounts began to merge the figure of the Ripper with literary characters from Gothic and sensation fiction, but also with tales of existing bogeyman figures that long before the 'autumn of terror' had kept children awake at nights and had found Victorian householders double-checking that they had bolted their back doors before retiring to bed.

## Jack's Forebears – Other Victorian Folk Devils and Bogeymen

The Ripper had at least two forbears in the Victorian imagination: the folk-devil 'Spring Heeled Jack' and, coming as a pair, the murderous and grave-robbing duo Burke and Hare. The latter are genuinely historical figures, only acquiring mythical associations after the exposure of their crimes and the execution of Burke and disappearance of Hare in 1828. In contrast, the origins of 'Spring Heeled Jack' are obscure: historical events may have played a part in his story, but superstition and legend quickly overtook whatever historical basis his stories may have had.

## Spring Heeled Jack

> Out of the darkness sprang a huge, cloaked figure. In an instant the man had thrown aside his cloak, revealing a hideous and frightful appearance. Blue and white flames vomited from his mouth, and his eyes appeared like balls of fire. The young girl who witnessed all this was so terrified she fainted right away.
>
> (*The Graphic*, August 1876)

This newspaper account of a late 19th-century sighting of 'Spring Heeled Jack' captures the essence of this bogeyman. By this date Jack was well known, with sightings having been reported over some 40 years. Each sighting followed a pattern: Spring Heeled Jack would spring from nowhere before a lone victim or occasionally small bands of travellers. He would scare and terrorize the victims, inciting panic, though generally he would not molest or assault them. The sightings, which took place in isolated parks or deserted urban streets, were widespread, cropping up across the United Kingdom. A good many occurred in London, the later stomping ground of the Ripper.

The origins of Spring Heeled Jack appear to lie in folklore, where he possibly fills an analogous function to the Roman God Pan, who would burst out upon

Two Victorian children play with a 'Jack in the Box', a more innocent take on the concept of a mischievous 'Jack' who springs from nowhere. (Mary Evans)

63

# THE LONDON MONSTER

The recent research of author Jan Bondeson has unearthed another semi-mythical figure whose dimly remembered reign of terror may also have tinged the treatment of the Ripper case in 1888. Known as 'The London Monster', this character was at large 100 years before the Whitechapel Murders and in the very different stalking ground of St James's Park in West London.

In a case that closely mirrors that of Spring Heeled Jack, 'The London Monster' terrorized a number of women in a series of attacks between 1788 and 1790. The attacks were verbal, mostly threats directed at women crossing the park, but they sometimes included the slashing and tearing of the clothing of the terrified victims. The Monster's crimes created a sensation in the London press, providing a dry run for the kind of hysteria that was to attend the Ripper murders a century later. While one Rhynwick Williams – who may or may not have been the culprit – was subsequently charged and found guilty of the crimes, the 'Monster' again seems to have outlived him as a bogeyman figure, and echoes of the case may just have reverberated all the way down to those paperboy's cries of 'Murder! Orrible Murder!' of 1888. The full story of these intriguing crimes is told by Jan Bondeson in The London Monster: Terror on the Streets in 1790, The History Press (London, 2005).

travellers wending their way through lonely places, inducing terror in them (and thereby providing the root of our modern word 'panic'). There are suggestive parallels too with the centuries-old child's toy, the Jack in the Box, where tension and surprise are intrinsic to the sudden bursting out of the concealed figure.

As the parallel with a child's toy would imply, there is something mischievous rather than entirely sinister about Spring Heeled Jack – as if he is an unruly rather than a malign force, a prankster more than a predator. He was certainly a nuisance, as witnesses this 1838 letter to Lord Mayor Sir John Cowan by a scandalized resident of South East London complaining of:

> some person who makes it his delight to frighten the peaceable inhabitants of the suburbs of the metropolis ... He has frightened several persons in Stockwell, Brixton, Camberwell and Vauxhall, and has caused the death of several; and many instances can be proved of his frightening people into fits.

The letter was one of several addressed to the mayor, who presided over a discussion in the Mansion House regarding this mysterious malefactor, variously referred to as a 'ghost', 'spectre', 'bear', and 'devil'. One prevalent theory suggested that Spring Heeled Jack was an individual of high rank (note the parallel with later Ripper theories) who was carrying out the series of scares as a bet.[8]

8. A full account of the Mansion House discussions is provided in the only full-length study of the figure yet to appear: Peter Haining's The Legend and Bizarre Crimes of Spring Heeled Jack, Frederick Mueller (London, 1977).

**OPPOSITE:**
The classic image of the Ripper, complete with top hat and Gladstone bag, is instantly recognizable - even though (or perhaps because) it owes more to fiction than reality.

Whatever his origins, Spring Heeled Jack had become a celebrated bogeyman figure by the Victorian era, featuring not only in stories relayed by oral tradition but also in 'penny dreadful' stories, where he increasingly took on the character of an anti-hero. In the autumn of 1888, when a killer burst suddenly out of the dark courts and alleyways in Whitechapel, wrought terror and violence, and promptly disappeared, the parallels between the two 'Jacks' would have been striking. Writing in 1929, Ripper author Leonard Matters recounted how the two figures had certainly been allied in his childhood imagination:

> As a mere baby, living 12,000 miles away from London, I heard the name of 'Jack the Ripper' and trembled in fear. It was synonymous in my infantile ears with something monstrous, horrible, spectral. It was used by other children in play when they wished to frighten one another. All they knew – all I knew at the time – was that somewhere there was a dreadful being who sprang, like the mythical companion of terror whom we associated with him – 'Spring-Heeled Jack' – out of dark alleys and from behind hedges, pounced upon his victims, man, woman, or child, and killed them. (*The Mystery of Jack the Ripper*, Chapter 2)

### Burke and Hare

The notorious events in Whitechapel 1888 were also tinged with the collective memory of unpleasant deeds in Edinburgh 1828. When Irish immigrants William Burke and William Hare discovered that Edinburgh surgeon Dr Robert Knox was in need of cadavers for his anatomical experiments and public lectures in dissection, they set about supplying this market in a most macabre manner. The pair progressed from stealing corpses to committing a series of 16 murders over a period of ten months.

The ghoulish activities of these 'bodysnatchers' made enough of an impression in their subsequent exposure and trial for their ghosts to loom over the inquest on second Ripper victim Annie Chapman 60 years later. Coroner Wynne Baxter's theory as to the motive for the murders was reported thus by *The Spectator* of 29 September 1888:

> [Coroner Baxter] has been the first to offer a reasonable explanation of the murders. They are atrocities of the old Burke and Hare type, aggravated. It appears that some American student of uterine pathology some months ago offered £20 each for specimens taken from corpses recently deceased. [ . . . ] The suggestion is that he [the murderer] had been tempted by the £20 as Burke was by the £7 10s offered for 'subjects', and has committed two murders to obtain the reward.

While, as we have seen, Baxter's theory was soon discredited, the incident provides a further striking example of the way in which the Ripper story, from the earliest stages, was heightened by association with these macabre tales and reminiscences of older vintage.

## The Ripper and the Gothic Novel

New stories of dark deeds and imaginings also played their part. By 1888 the tradition of the Gothic novel was well established. Extending back at least as far as Horace Walpole's 1764 novel *The Castle of Otranto*, the Gothic literary tradition delighted in tales of peril, mystery, and suspense, typically set in dark and isolated settings. The tradition had been given new impetus in the Victorian era by such works as Edgar Allen Poe's *The Murders in the Rue Morgue* and by the 'penny dreadful' sub-genre of fiction. It is certainly a striking coincidence just how many of the classics of the Victorian Gothic literature tradition appeared within a decade years of the Whitechapel Murders: Stevenson's *Strange Case of Dr Jekyll and Mr Hyde* in 1886; Conan Doyle's first Sherlock Holmes novel, *A Study in Scarlet*, in 1887; Wilde's *The Picture of Dorian Gray* in 1890; Bram Stoker's *Dracula* in 1897. Snippets from any one of these novels summon images of the Ripper legend. Consider, for example, the description of Count Dracula leering at a potential victim at Piccadilly Circus in London:

> a tall, thin man, with a beaky nose and black moustache and pointed beard, who was also observing the pretty girl [ . . . ] His face was not a good face; it was hard, and cruel, and sensual, and his big white teeth, that looked all the whiter because his lips were so red, were pointed like an animal's.
>
> (*Dracula*, Chapter 13)

**OVERLEAF**

Richard Mansfield's nightly portrayal of Jekyll and Hyde at London's Lyceum Theatre during the Ripper's reign of terror provided an eerie artistic counterpoint to the events unfolding in Whitechapel and left an indelible impression on how the crimes were reported and remembered.

Consider too the scene from Oscar Wilde's *The Picture of Dorian Gray* when, as observed by Ripper author Thomas Toughill, the protagonist spies his friend Basil Hallward prowling the London streets on 9 November (the date of Mary Jane Kelly's murder) in garb that is clearly redolent of the Ripper:

> He was walking home about eleven o'clock from Lord Henry's, where he had been dining, and was wrapped in heavy furs, as the night was cold and foggy. At the corner of Grosvenor Square and South Audley Street a man passed him in the mist, walking very fast, and with the collar of his grey ulster turned up. He had a bag in his hand. Dorian recognized him. It was Basil Hallward. A strange sense of fear, for which he could not account, came over him.
>
> (*The Picture of Dorian Gray*, Chapter 12)[9]

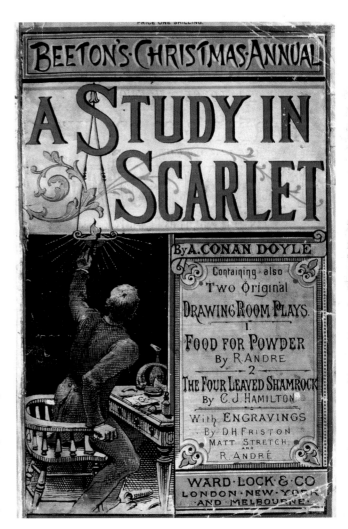

Threads in the textual web surrounding the story of Jack the Ripper. Sir Arthur Conan Doyle's first Sherlock Holmes story, *A Study in Scarlet* (left), appeared the year before the Whitechapel Murders, (Mary Evans)

However, where art and life parallels in the Ripper story reached their zenith was in the extraordinary collision that took place that autumn between the true events unfolding in Whitechapel in the autumn of 1888 and a stage adaptation of Robert Louis Stevenson's dark tale of Dr Jekyll and Mr Hyde.

Robert Louis Stevenson's short novel of 1886 had explored the concept of the split personality – the troubling notion that an apparently upstanding and responsible member of society could house a 'dark side', transforming into a monstrous and predatory figure when away from the gaze of respectable society. Dr Jekyll's transformation into the bestial Edward Hyde is initially wrought whenever he drinks a mysterious potion concocted in his laboratory, but before long the dark side takes over and transformation into Hyde becomes involuntary.

This troubling image of the face of respectability being a mask for inner monstrosity resonated with the late Victorians, and Stevenson's novel was sufficiently popular to be adapted into a stage play that opened in New York before transferring to London. In one of the most remarkable instances of art

---

9. For Toughill's theory that Wilde's novel is a coded account of the Whitechapel Murders, see *The Ripper Code*, The History Press (Stroud, 2008).

Dr Jekyll stalks the London streets and claims another victim.

imitating life, this stage adaptation of *The Strange Case of Dr Jekyll and Mr Hyde* began playing on the London stage just as the Jack the Ripper murders began. Opening on 5 August 1888, the production featured actor Richard Mansfield as both Jekyll and Hyde, his onstage transformation from gentleman to monster leaving an indelible impression on those who witnessed it.

From a very early stage in the reporting of the Whitechapel Murders, the factual Ripper and fictional Hyde became merged. *The Freeman's Journal* suggested 'these atrocities and apparently causeless murders show that there is abroad at the present time in the East End a human monster even more terrible than Hyde', while *The Pall Mall Gazette* even ran the headline, 'Mr Hyde at large in Whitechapel'. A correspondent writing to *The Star* proposed that 'The murderer is a Mr Hyde, who seeks in the repose and comparative respectability of Dr Jekyll security from the crimes he commits in his baser shape'. Other commentators suggested that the onstage portrayal of dark deeds might be inspiring the killer, while one correspondent to the police even suggested that Richard Mansfield himself was the Ripper.

Things came to a head in late September 1888 when the closure of the play was announced. *The Telegraph* reported the closure in words that summed up just how eerie the parallels between art and life had become that autumn: 'There is no taste just now for horrors on the stage. There is quite sufficient to make us shudder out of doors'.[10]

## Completing the Transformation: The Lodger and Later Ripper Novels

Thus, in 1892, when the Scotland Yard investigation of the murders was winding down, the journey of Jack the Ripper from fearsome real-life criminal to *dramatis persona* was already well under way. The historical Whitechapel Murderer had already begun to merge with a whole spectrum of characters from folk devil Spring Heeled Jack to literary fiend Edward Hyde. This transition from fact to fiction was completed by novelist Marie Belloc Lowndes in 1911 with the serialized publication in *McClure's Magazine* of her novel, *The Lodger*. A chance conversation at a dinner party started it all, as Belloc Lowndes subsequently related in her diary:

> I heard a man telling a woman at a dinner party that his mother had had a butler and a cook who married and kept lodgers. They were convinced that Jack the Ripper had spent a night under their roof.

The premise fired the novelist's imagination, and thus she began to pen her tale of Robert and Ellen Bunting, a late middle aged couple whose reliable former careers in service have given way to reduced circumstances,

---

10. There may be traces of Jekyll and Hyde even in those most authoritative of Ripper historical documents, the MacNaughten Memoranda, where Sir Melville describes Montague John Druitt as a professional man 'of good family' who conceals a dark side and who is suspected of the murders by his own relatives. Druitt's profession is wrongly given as 'doctor'.

advertising for lodgers in their house in Marylebone. Huddled around their parlour fire, curtains drawn against the cold and fog, the pair hear the cries of paperboys announcing 'Horrible Murder! Murder at St Pancras!' and are steadily drawn into a saga of serial murder, first by their own morbid interest in following the case in the press, and subsequently by their suspicion of the urbane lodger who takes rooms in their house, keeping odd hours and following eccentric habits. He arrives, of course, on a foggy night, carrying only one item of luggage – a leather bag.

# MADAME TUSSAUD'S

### EXHIBITION, BAKER STREET, W.

# CHRISTMAS NOVELTIES.

A GRAND GROUP, REPRESENTING, IN GORGEOUS ASIATIC COSTUMES,

## The Various Princes and Dignitaries of Her Majesty's Indian Empire.

### ALSO SHERE ALI.

The GOVERNOR-GENERAL of CANADA, The Most Noble the MARQUIS OF LORNE, and H.R.H. PRINCESS LOUISE.

## A MAGNIFICENT REPRESENTATION OF THE BERLIN CONGRESS, &C., &C.

### ENTIRE RENOVATION OF THE CHAMBER OF HORRORS.

#### THE GALLOWS.

*This actual GALLOWS, just acquired at* MADAME TUSSAUD AND SONS', *we should mention that it has been put to its terrible use now for upwards of fifty years, and who knows how many agonized souls it has silently launched into eternity? The GALLOWS itself is a perfect piece of destructive ingenuity, and must be seen for its fearful aptitude to be fully understood, and the drop would make the most callous turn cold to contemplate. There is also a temporary platform, with a falling leaf supported by bolts, upon which the wretched culprit is placed, and these are so perfectly, though ominously fixed, that in an instant they swerve and the victim is launched into eternity. Not a crevice is there for escape, not a weakness anywhere for failure. "The wages of sin is death," has been for fifty years the motto under which this thing has done its appalling work of expiation. It now stands at rest at* MADAME TUSSAUD'S *beside its sister, the French Guillotine. The sight of this thing tells in unspeakable words how terrible is the punishment of crime more forcibly than the most eloquent homily that was ever uttered. It is now an historical record of the greatest value.*

#### ADMISSION 1s.

Children under Twelve, 6d.    Extra Rooms, 6d.    Open from 10 a.m. till 10 p.m.
*Travellers by Metropolitan Railway stop at Baker Street Station.*

An 1876 poster announces the revamp of Madame Tussaud's Chamber of Horrors, now boasting the addition of a genuine gallows that had been employed in executions for over 50 years. Perhaps in acknowledgement of how theatrical the Ripper story had become, the denouement of *The Lodger* is played out not on the London streets but in the shadows of the Chamber of Horrors, amongst the waxwork effigies of murderers past. (Mary Evans)

Belloc Lowndes' novel is largely responsible for the more sanitized, 'stage villain' image of the Ripper that stays with us to this day. The book's settings are largely domestic and familiar, and trips to the outside world are centred on excursions to such venues as Scotland Yard's Black Museum or Madame Tussaud's Chamber of Horrors, where crime is collected and exhibited as a curiosity and viewed at a safe distance. The novel also transposes the horrific series of Ripper killings into a lighter key: the murders take place in the West End rather than the deprived East; the victims are partakers of the demon drink rather than sisters of the night; the Ripper is renamed 'the Avenger' and his motivation is religious mania rather than sadism. It is no accident that we are introduced to protagonist Bunting as he languishes comfortably in his armchair – for it is the Ripper story as armchair thriller that Belloc Lowndes bequeaths us, best read in the comforting glow of a warming fire.

*The Lodger* shows the Buntings, like all of us, simultaneously enthralled and horrified by their morbid curiosity in serial murder. When Bunting reads sections of the paper to his wife over breakfast, 'in spite of herself Mrs Bunting had felt thrilled and excited' (Chapter 4), while elsewhere Bunting protests,

'I don't think I'm a bloodthirsty man! But I'm just terribly interested in all that sort of thing – always have been'. (Chapter 8) As the 125 years of international interest in Jack the Ripper show, Bunting is by no means alone.

Thus it was that the figure of Jack the Ripper completed the transformation from real life criminal to fictional character. From the early press accounts of his crimes onwards, the figure of the Whitechapel Murderer was merged and mingled with figures from folklore, Gothic literature, and melodrama until, bizarrely, he was more imagined than real. Just as the present day owners of 221b Baker Street are regularly obliged to advise tourists that Sherlock Holmes did not in fact exist, so we sometimes need to stop and remind ourselves that Jack the Ripper most certainly did.

## The Victims' Tales

Some Ripper-themed literature has rightly sought to tell more of the story of the women whose tragic deaths lie at the heart of the mystery. Anna Robinson's poems 'Portraits of Women – East London – 1888' focus poignantly on the specific details associated with these women's last days and deeds, and on what is known of their family lives. The portrait of Annie Chapman is representative of the gentle tone and eye for detail in each of the sketches:

> Her movements are, eventually, always easterly. Steady, sturdy, she walks, always circling that idea, with a good wide stride. Her face is round. Her eyes are blue. Her dark brown hair is curly. It holds pins tolerably. Her fringe is thick and long. Her lips are full. She is pale. She is dying and will do what she wants. Crochet, she loves to crochet – but where is the hook? She does not drink except for rum. She moves with the ghost of a young girl beside her. Her son is a cripple. Her daughter has run away to the circus. The fences along Hanbury Street are five feet tall. She is five feet tall. *See that Tim keeps the bed for me.* Twenty-nine is her favourite number. She always sleeps at number twenty-nine.

# CHAPTER SEVEN: CAUGHT ON FILM

Our tracing of the Ripper's trail ends at the only place he was ever caught – on film. The iconic figure of the Ripper was always going to translate well to film and television, and in these media he has endured as successfully as in print. First there was Alfred Hitchcock's 1927 silent film version of Marie Belloc Lowndes's *The Lodger, now subtitled by the director* 'A Story of the London Fog'. Starring 1920s matinée idol Ivor Novello, the film portrayed the classic

Dr Watson (James Mason), Inspector Lestrade (Frank Finlay) and an increasingly determined Sherlock Holmes (Christopher Plummer) visit Mitre Square on the night of the double murder. (Moviestore Collection Ltd / Alamy)

Lewis Collins and Michael Caine's Godley and Abberline stand vigil at the entrance to Miller's Court in the 1988 television film *Jack the Ripper*. (AF Archive / Alamy)

'Gentleman Jack' image of the Ripper. The lodger emerges from the London fog complete with hat, cloak, and Gladstone bag; in a further sinister touch added by Hitchcock, the killer's apparel now includes a scarf concealing the mouth and drawing the audience's focus to the blank, expressionless eyes.

The film's famous set pieces include the admission of the lodger into the house against a backdrop of swirling fog, and the unnerving cross-cutting between shots of the increasingly suspicious and fearful landlady's face and the pacing and prowling of the lodger through the upper rooms of the house.

Produced in the same year as *The Lodger*, the silent Hollywood film *London After Midnight* featured Lon Chaney, star of Gothic dramas *The Hunchback of Notre Dame* (1923) and *The Phantom of the Opera* (1925), as a character closely modelled on the popular image of Jack the Ripper. The film is today thought to be lost, only a selection of stills and press photographs remaining, but the haunting images that do exist are a powerful testament to how the 'Gentleman Jack' image of the Ripper had seared itself into the popular consciousness within 50 years of the murders having been committed.

When the Ripper story was retold in the 1958 film *Jack the Ripper*, these classic images of 'Gentleman Jack' were again to the fore, showing how indispensable the top hat, cape, and Gladstone bag had become in the imagery associated with the character.

Yet the story of 'the killer who got away' could potentially make for a rather one-sided drama. In terms of dramatic storytelling, the Ripper needed a nemesis. What better figure than the equally iconic Sherlock Holmes? The combination of these two characters proved irresistible and resulted in two films, 1965's *A Study in Terror* and 1979's *Murder by Decree*, which both pitted Sherlock Holmes and the faithful Dr Watson against the dreaded Ripper.

Unmasking the killer in their final reels, the films portray the 'Gentleman Jack' and conspiracy theories of the murders respectively.

Two other Ripper films of the 1970s add twists of fantasy and the supernatural to the story. In the 1971 Hammer horror film *Hands of the Ripper*, the killer's daughter becomes possessed by her father's murderous spirit, while in the 1979 adventure *Time after Time*, the Ripper's escape from the Victorian police is explained by his use of a time machine, invented by science fiction novelist H. G. Wells, which he uses to transport himself to late 20th-century San Francisco.

Having set both Sherlock Holmes and H. G. Wells on the heels of the Ripper, film treatments turned next to the genuine historical detective who had sought him, Frederick George Abberline. A television film prepared for airing on the centenary of the murders in 1988 featured Michael Caine as a heavy drinking but determined inspector of H Division, ably assisted by

A scene from the 2001 film *From Hell*, in which Johnny Depp's Abberline hunts the Ripper and reveals a conspiracy. (AF archive / Almay)

Lewis Collins's Sergeant Godley. The tale of their quest for the Ripper nodded at both the conspiracy theories and the deranged doctor theories that had been so prevalent in the Ripper literature over the previous 15 years.

Abberline was also the protagonist of the 2001 film *From Hell*, based upon Alan Moore's graphic novel of 1999. Now portrayed by Johnny Depp, this Abberline hunts the Ripper not only on the mean streets of the East End but in the corners of his own mind during drug induced visions and hallucinations. He eventually unearths a malign conspiracy behind the crimes – though one that in this version of events fails to claim the life of final Ripper victim Mary Jane Kelly, who escapes Whitechapel for a new life.

In recent years, Ripper-themed film and television has focused less on retelling the Ripper tale than on exploiting the 'shadows of the Ripper' or his legacy in the annals of crime. Thus the ITV drama *Whitechapel* portrays a team of East End detectives employing both forensic methods and a knowledge of classic crime to solve modern copycat crimes in London, while the BBC period drama *Ripper Street* depicts the H Division men who would have brushed shoulders with Abberline policing a volatile Whitechapel and Spitalfields in the years immediately after the Ripper scare.

It is interesting to speculate where the Ripper might materialize next. At the time of this book going to press, leaked photographs from the set of long-running science fiction drama *Doctor Who* suggest that the time-travelling doctor will soon be on the trail of the Whitechapel Murderer. If the Ripper should escape capture by travelling through time, it will only be the latest step in his long journey from fact to fiction, true crime to tall tale, history to imagination.

# FURTHER READING AND ACKNOWLEDGEMENTS

There are now so many texts published on the Ripper that it would be a life's work to read them all – and not always time well spent. The truly indispensable books on the subject are fewer in number. They include:

Begg, Paul, Martin Fido, and Keith Skinner, *The Complete Jack the Ripper A–Z*, John Blake (London, 2010), first published as *The Jack the Ripper A-Z* (1991).

Knight, Stephen, *Jack the Ripper: The Final Solution*, Harper Collins (London, 1975; repr. 2010).

Rumbelow, Donald, *The Complete Jack the Ripper*, revised updated edition, Virgin Books (London, 2013).

Sugden, Philip, *A Complete History of Jack the Ripper*, 2nd revised edition, Robinson (London, 2002).

Whittington-Egan, Richard, *Jack the Ripper: The Definitive Casebook*, Amberley Publishing (Stroud, 2013).

As for the future of Ripper studies, the really interesting direction of travel is the exploration of the crimes in the light of the historical, cultural, and literary contexts of late Victorian Britain. Excellent books in this vein include:

Flanders, Judith, *The Invention of Murder: How the Victorians Revelled in Death and Detection and Created Modern Crime*, Harper Press (London, 2011).

Worsley, Lucy, *A Very British Murder*, Random House (London, 2013).

## Acknowledgements

Lucy Worsley is surely right in observing that the facts in the Ripper case are 'rather grubby and shop-soiled from so much handling'. For their faith that even now these facts might be viewed in a fresh light, I am grateful to Joseph McCullough and Rufus Thurston of Osprey Publishing.

The Ripper tale is a tragic one, but I hope for the most part we retell it not to dwell on violence and suffering but to affirm the quest for intrigue in the human imagination. Such a spirit certainly motivates the friends and colleagues with whom I have discussed the case for approaching 30 years: Ross Andrews, Jill Barke, Sergeant Paul Gathercole, Joanne Larter,

Kathryn Luke-Taylor and Matthew Percival. My thanks to them and also to Martin Fido who very generously read and commented on the manuscript (any errors remain emphatically my own);Anna Robinson for permission to quote from 'Portraits of Women –East London – 1888'; Dr Matthew Pearson who proofread the manuscript with an expert eye; Dr Emma Plaskitt, whose deep knowledge of Gothic and sensation novels opened up valuable directions; Martin Nichols, who alerted me to an important literary source; Abraham Davies and Dr Hugh Gazzard for tonal pointers; and the late Dr Nick Kneale, who enabled me to explore some of the book's ideas in lectures at Oxford.

The book is dedicated to James Dalrymple, who picked out the first study of the case I ever read and who, more than anyone, can tell the Gothic from the ghoulish.

- Victor Stapleton, St Ives, Cornwall (February 2014)